# PRAISE FOR *LET THE WORLD SEE YOU*

"In a world with too many fakes, Sam Acho is the real deal. I consider myself fortunate to have gotten to know him, and I am honored to call him a friend. This book reveals the real Sam Acho, and we are all the better for that revelation."

—GEORGE H. MCCASKEY, CHAIRMAN OF THE CHICAGO BEARS

"Not everyone has the strength to live out loud, to be honest with the world about who they really are. Sam is leading us to freedom by being an example. This is a must-read."

—LECRAE, GRAMMY-WINNING ARTIST, ACTOR, AND *NEW YORK TIMES* BESTSELLING AUTHOR

"I'm so glad that you are holding a copy of *Let the World See You* in your hands. Sam Acho is an exceptional man, whose desire to honor God and influence others is an inspiration. I've known him since we were elementary age and have always admired his commitment to integrity, pursuit of authenticity, and passion for excellence in every area of life. In each chapter, these characteristics come shining through as he shares personal details from his own experience underscored by sound Biblical insight. When you turn the last page, you'll be equipped with the courage you need to exchange the exhaustion of performance-based living for the freedom and joy of being exactly who God has created you to be. This book is worth reading. Enjoy!"

—PRISCILLA SHIRER, BIBLE TEACHER AND AUTHOR

"There are few voices and authors that the world needs as desperately as Sam's right now. He is a voice of wisdom, humility, truth, and prophetic witness that everyone can learn from together on this journey of being human. I am beyond grateful for this book and will be buying ten and giving them out!"

—JEFFERSON BETHKE, *NEW YORK TIMES* BESTSELLING AUTHOR OF *JESUS > RELIGION* AND *TO HELL WITH THE HUSTLE*

"Sam Acho is a trusted voice in my life, and this is how I decide that: when someone lives what they teach, the best days and the hard ones too, I trust them. Sam has done this in the pages of this book. He has let the world see him, and it gives me new courage to let the world see me too."

—ANNIE F. DOWNS, BESTSELLING AUTHOR AND
HOST OF *THAT SOUNDS FUN* PODCAST

"Take a journey with Sam Acho as he laughs, cries, and completely lets his guard down to give you a glimpse into the person he is at his core. When you do, I know you will be inspired to do the same. I've been fortunate to know Sam for a long, long time, and he has always been conscientious in his actions and sincere in his work. In *Let the World See You*, Sam offers unique insight on what it means to be seen, to be known, and to be human. It is for EVERYONE. Thank you, Sam, for being so vulnerable and letting the world see YOU. This is an authentic look at what it means to be real, and I'm excited for people to read this book and be inspired by its message."

—COACH MACK BROWN

"I know one of the most difficult things in life, no matter what stage you are in, is to figure out who you are, or maybe more importantly, who you want to be. Then once you figure this out, it can be equally difficult to gain the confidence and courage to share that person with the world. *Let the World See You* is full of inspiring stories, encouraging us to discover who we are and to never be afraid of sharing that person with others. Sam dives into how—through relationships with family, friends, and Jesus—he became convinced of who he was created to be and what he was created for: to be a world changer. He lets us know that such title is not simply set aside for a few, like him, it is reserved for each and every one of us. But the only way to live up to this title is by being your true self, by being YOU. I believe after reading this book you will want to set off on your own journey to discover who God created you to be, and how, with His help, little, old YOU can change the world. *Let the World See You* is a must-read for anyone who is struggling to figure out their identity, and for those who have figured it out but are afraid to let that person loose because they're not sure the world will like who they are. Sam, like most of us, struggled with both of these things, but once he figured them out there was no stopping him. And he wants you to know the same can be true for you."

—KURT WARNER, NFL HALL-OF-FAME QUARTERBACK

"Sam Acho is one of those rare multitalented young men who have successfully married technical excellence and spiritual maturity. In this fine, inspiring, and insightful book, Sam challenges all of us to live authentic lives worth being emulated. Read, embrace, and absorb his words if you are serious about living a genuine life."

—DR. TONY EVANS, PRESIDENT OF THE URBAN ALTERNATIVE
AND SENIOR PASTOR OF OAK CLIFF BIBLE FELLOWSHIP

"I've been friends with Sam for some years now. I'd go to his games when he was in town, and he'd always come to my shows when I was in his city. Through the years we developed a friendship, and to this day we call each other to talk about life, faith, work, and marriage. When you see a six-foot-four, muscled linebacker, you don't typically think gentle, kind, or vulnerable. But those are the words I'd use to describe Sam. Every time we talk, he shares what's on his heart. We celebrate the good and don't shy away from the bad. Sam is honest about his missteps and uncertainty, and even invites critique. I've always admired that. It takes a strong person to be vulnerable and do what seems weak in our culture. In entertainment and in sports, it's rare to find genuine people who can leave their profession at the door and be real with you. I value my friendship with Sam because being an NFL player is what he does, not who he is. When we talk, I get

Sam Acho the person, not the persona. I'm excited for this book because you'll get to see that person too. Sam has many more talents besides hitting people. And with his gift of writing, he shares the wisdom he has accumulated over the years. I know this book will bless you!"

—ANDY MINEO, HIP-HOP AND RECORDING ARTIST

"Sam has written one of the most open, honest, and impactful books I've ever read about a professional athlete. His unique ability to simplify the Bible helps us to understand who God is and how to apply Bible stories to positively impact our own lives and others. Showing vulnerability is difficult for anyone, especially someone constantly in the public eye, but Sam's willingness to share his true thoughts and feelings brings us directly into his life. People from all walks of life and from every faith can relate to this story. It will leave you feeling more self-confident, knowing that many people have overcome the same struggles and adversity you may be facing."

—PAUL GOLDSCHMIDT, FIRST BASEMAN FOR THE
ST. LOUIS CARDINALS AND SIX-TIME MLB ALL-STAR

"Sam Acho's vulnerable, authentic words inspired a renewed call in me to love people deeply and listen boldly, and to seek and follow Jesus. Sam's unwavering character in both prosperous and challenging times shines through in a raw, refreshing way that continually points readers to God."

—GARY A. HAUGEN, FOUNDER AND CEO OF
INTERNATIONAL JUSTICE MISSION

let the world
# see
# you

# let the world
# see
# you

## How to Be Real in a
## World Full of Fakes

### SAM ACHO

NELSON
BOOKS

An Imprint of Thomas Nelson

Published in Nashville, Tennessee, by Nelson Books, an imprint of Thomas Nelson. Nelson Books and Thomas Nelson are registered trademarks of HarperCollins Christian Publishing, Inc.

Published in association with The Bindery Agency, www.TheBinderyAgency.com.

Thomas Nelson titles may be purchased in bulk for educational, business, fundraising, or sales promotional use. For information, please e-mail SpecialMarkets@ThomasNelson.com.

### Library of Congress Cataloging-in-Publication Data

Names: Acho, Sam, 1988- author.
Title: Let the world see you : how to be real in a world full of fakes / Sam Acho.
Description: Nashville, Tennessee : Nelson Books, [2020] | Summary: "NFL linebacker, speaker, podcaster, and humanitarian Sam Acho gives a blueprint for taking off our masks and living lives of genuine authenticity"--Provided by publisher.
Identifiers: LCCN 2020007531 (print) | LCCN 2020007532 (ebook) | ISBN 9781400220274 (hardcover) | ISBN 9781400220458 (ebook)
Subjects: LCSH: Acho, Sam, 1988- | Football players--United States--Biography. | Self-acceptance--Religious aspects--Christianity. | Self-esteem--Religious aspects--Christianity.
Classification: LCC GV939.A37 A3 2020 (print) | LCC GV939.A37 (ebook) | DDC 796.332092 [B]--dc23
LC record available at https://lccn.loc.gov/2020007531
LC ebook record available at https://lccn.loc.gov/2020007532

*Printed in the United States of America*

20 21 22 23 24  LSC  10 9 8 7 6 5 4 3 2 1

*To Jerry Price.*
*Thank you for sharing with me what life is all about.*

# CONTENTS

# CONTENTS

# FOREWORD

History's great sculptor Michelangelo had a really profound way of approaching his craft. It's been recorded that he said, "Every block of stone has a statue inside it, and it is the task of the sculptor to discover it." And about his *Angel*, "I saw the angel in the marble and carved until I set him free."

In many ways, the same is true of us. Within each of us is an amazing piece of art that has been shaped, formed, and crafted by the great Artist. And he desperately desires to set us free.

We all like the sound of that, of course, but it can feel impossible to believe that it's true. *Sure, we think, for the famous person, the shiny social media influencer, the mom down the street who always seems perfectly put together, the coworker getting promoted, the athlete making play after play, or the business leader driving the new luxury car.* It's easy to see them as works of art to be celebrated and adored. But if we're honest, it can be difficult to look in the mirror and see the same potential in ourselves. Sometimes it takes the words of another to chip away at our insecurities and fears to speak the art into being.

When I met Sam Acho for the first time in a back room of a sushi restaurant outside Chicago, I had no idea it would lead to a lifelong friendship. He reached out, and we set up a time to connect. But I really had no idea why he wanted to meet or what he wanted to discuss. As a pastor, I should add that this scenario isn't unusual as I have the honor of meeting with people often, and I absolutely love the pastoral connections that can occur during those conversations. We sat together for two hours and covered everything from faith to failure to marriages to hopes to worries for the future. The time flew by, something I have come to learn was always the case with Sam. He has a way of making you feel right at home, just as you are, every time. As I drove away, I was especially struck by Sam's honesty and humility, which felt so refreshing in an environment where that takes extensive courage and intentionality.

A few weeks later, a friend who coaches basketball for a college down the road from that sushi restaurant invited me to hoop with him and some friends, a few of whom turned out to be Sam and other Chicago Bears players. I brought my son to the game, who was happy to observe from the stands while playing with his current obsession: Pokémon cards. What stands out to me about that day is that between games, Sam sat with my son and peppered him with questions about Pokémon. He saw my son sitting there, not really being into sports, and found a way to connect with him by seeing what he was excited about. I'll never forget my son's words at bedtime that night. He rolled over and told me, "Mr. Acho really likes Pokémon, and I sure liked talking to him."

In a few short weeks, I witnessed a man who was physically strong but even stronger in his intentional care for others. It's almost as if with each conversation Sam was gently chiseling away, making space for my son (and me) to feel free enough and safe enough to be fully seen.

Over the years, I've watched Sam do this time and time again. With business leaders, teammates, and pastors, with those who are struggling, with those who are incarcerated, with kids and college students—basically, with pretty much every person he encounters.

After hearing his story, I understand more than ever why this message of acceptance so deeply matters to him. When you've been set free, why would you still want to hide? When you've been created for a purpose, why would you want to pretend to be something you're not?

Recently I drove past a massive slab of marble, and I wondered aloud, "What if Michelangelo chose to not see *David* or *Pietà*? What if he never picked up the chisel and start chipping away?" Michelangelo would have missed out. The entire art community would have missed out. The entire world would have missed out.

The same goes for you.

This book is Sam taking his life—all the defining moments that God used to chisel away at his fears, wounds, and insecurities—and stepping into who he was always meant to be. Let Sam guide you and show you what it means to be you, to be seen and known. Let him help you discover how this new way of living will not only bless you but also bless those around you, and yes, even the world.

Let the crafting and sculpting begin.

*Steve Carter*

# INTRODUCTION

## *You Are Worth Getting to Know*

Just recently I lost a friend. I'm not sure if loss or death has been a part of your life, but it has most certainly *not* been a part of mine. Prior to this loss, I had only ever attended one funeral: a friend's father. Though my friend and I didn't know each other too well, he asked me to be a pallbearer, and of course I obliged.

This time, however, was different. Several years ago, when we were living in Phoenix, some new neighbors moved in next door to us. Jerry and Judy Price had been married for more than forty years, and yet they looked like they were still in love as they held hands, danced together, and threw parties for their friends. They had married young, at ages twenty and nineteen, and had been enjoying life together ever since. I wanted that kind of relationship. My wife, Ngozi, and I had just celebrated our one-year anniversary, and quite frankly, we were just trying to figure it all out.

God couldn't have given us better neighbors, and Judy

immediately connected with Ngozi. My wife had recently moved to the States from Nigeria, and making friends had proven difficult.

"Americans," Ngozi said, "are too fast-paced. Always on the go."

But she found Judy to be different. Judy would sit with her friends, invite them over often, and get to know them. As a result, she and Ngozi became great friends.

Jerry became more than a friend to me; he became a mentor. I would often sneak over to his house and just sit with him, abide in his presence, and be excited to receive a few words of wisdom. I always learned something because Jerry was different from most men. His personality was in-your-face and confident and yet, at the same time, caring, thoughtful, and compassionate. He reminded me of my dad. Jerry was also dashing and charming, so it was no surprise he had married a woman like Judy. We often joked that he had married way above his level, or as I put it, "Outkicked his coverage." Jerry was also fearless. He would call you out if he felt it was necessary and still love you through whatever circumstance or situation. That was why it hurt so much when I received a call from Jerry asking for permission to go.

Jerry had fought a yearslong battle with cancer, and he had done everything imaginable to get better. Nothing worked. He had lost weight as well as his appetite, and he had finally reached a point where he was ready to see Jesus. When we spoke, he explained to me that he was in a good place with God and felt it was his time to go home. That's when he asked for my blessing to leave.

In that moment I was confused and sad. I didn't understand why he wasn't getting better. I didn't understand why the treatments weren't working. To be frank, I didn't understand why Jerry was asking for my permission.

You see, I had moved to Chicago from Phoenix years ago. Jerry and I talked often during those years, but we were no longer living next door to each other. My mind spun. Why did he need my permission? Why did he even ask? The reason is that Jerry was a gentleman, and he knew an important truth I had yet to realize: his life was not his own. His life was for others, and I was one of those others in his life. Jerry had impacted me in ways too deep to explain with words. I believe God placed him in my life for a specific purpose and at a specific time, and he blessed my life tremendously. So when Jerry asked for my permission to go, I said yes. But I also needed something from him before he left.

I asked him for a few final words of wisdom. I needed a little more of the guidance I knew only he could give.

"If you could tell me anything," I began, "anything about what you know about me or about life, what would it be?"

I had learned to wait with Jerry, so I waited patiently to hear his carefully measured and thereafter treasured words of wisdom. Then he spoke, but with only a fraction of the former strength in his voice.

"I have two thoughts for you, Sam," he said. "In my seventy-one years of life, I've learned one thing: Jesus wants to be known. *Intimately.* He takes joy in our getting to know him. Knowing him is more precious than anything money can buy. Get to know Jesus intimately," he said.

I paused to take in what he said, but I was also eager to hear Jerry's next advice.

"You are worth getting to know, Sam," he said. "Never forget that."

Those would be the last words I ever heard from my dear friend. Three days later Jerry slipped into a coma and died peacefully at his home. I had flown back to see him but arrived just a few minutes too late.

I walked into the house and saw Judy. I gave her a big hug. I then sat with her and her family, listening to them tell stories about the man I called my mentor. I learned much about Jerry that day. I learned about his character, his heart, and his sense of humor. But those ten words he'd said to me just a few days before could not escape my mind: *You are worth getting to know, Sam. Never forget that.*

This book is about what it means to be known, and by extension, what it means to be human. It's about what it means to *be*. I now know and believe I am worth getting to know. And I believe you are too. Not for your benefit alone, but for the benefit of the people around you, including your friends, your family, your neighbors, and those people you have yet to meet. Let the world see you. Your quirks, your fears, your kindness, your courage. You were not meant to hide. You were made to be seen and loved.

Nelson Mandela is known to have said:

Our deepest fear is not that we are inadequate. Our deepest fear is that we are powerful beyond measure. It is our light, not our darkness, that most frightens us. We ask ourselves, Who am I to be brilliant, gorgeous, talented, and fabulous? Actually, who are you *not* to be? You are a child of God. Your playing small doesn't serve the world. There's nothing enlightened about shrinking so that other people won't feel insecure around you. We are all meant to shine, as children do. We were born to make manifest the glory of God that is within us. It's not just in some of us; it's in everyone. And as we let our own light shine, we unconsciously give other people permission to do the same. As we're liberated from our own fear, our presence automatically liberates others.[1]

**Let the world see you.**

In this book you will read about times when I hid, times when I was too scared to let the world see me. Pain usually ensued. But you'll also read about times when I heeded my friend's advice and allowed myself to be seen, and about the joy and freedom that followed. Let the world see you. Let the world know you. Why? Because you are worth getting to know.

# chapter one

# HIDING

At one point or another we all face times when our insecurities flare up directly in front of us. In these moments we are left to choose between one of three options: address the insecurities, run from them, or hide from them.

When I was younger, my natural instinct was to choose the third option.

Hiding has always been the easy option for me. Whenever I came across a situation I wasn't comfortable in, I would simply find a way to escape. I would find a place to hide. The problem arose when that temporary hiding place became a permanent one.

One night, at age thirteen, I was attending the Wednesday evening youth service as usual, at our predominantly black church. My dad was one of the pastors of this relatively large congregation, and by default I always tried not to be noticed. But this night would be different. I thought I was the Man in a red Tommy Hilfiger shirt, a pair of reversible blue Nautica shorts, and a brand-new pair of purple FUBU shoes. You see, the school I attended outfitted all the students in uniforms, and my weekend attire usually consisted of random combinations of basketball shorts and T-shirts. So on this night, I was quite proud of my new digs. But even though it was church, people are people, and some people tend to be mean. Especially to little kids who're trying hard to impress.

Wednesday night services for the youth at my church were different. The first forty-five minutes were spent with junior high and high school grades together. So kids from twelve to eighteen years old were all in the same room. Then, for the last half of the service, we were split up into age groups. This last half of the service was fine for me, as I was a thirteen-year-old among my peers. It was the first forty-five minutes I dreaded.

Being thirteen was hard enough, featuring voice cracks, awkward growth spurts, and acne. Puberty had started doing its work on me, but what made it even harder was being around opinionated high schoolers. When they saw my outfit that night, they did not hold back.

"Bro, what are you wearing?" several of the guys asked.

"Who dressed you? Do you even know how to wear clothes?" they continued.

"Oh, you thought you was fly? You thought wrong! Who is this kid?"

I was thoroughly roasted. I was crushed.

In the African American community, poking fun at someone for their attire or their speech is commonplace. But because I went to a predominately white school and had grown up in a Nigerian household, I wasn't used to this kind of roasting. So when these high school kids began poking fun at me and my clothes, it devastated me. But the comments that followed were even worse.

"Oh, you know who that is, right?" one said to his friends. "That's Dr. Acho's son. You can't talk about him."

The words cut like knives. Everyone knew my dad and loved him. He was gregarious, full of energy, and the last person to leave the building after every service. And here I was, his thirteen-year-old son, who everyone knew for the wrong reasons. I was ashamed, and I ran and hid.

My hiding place at church was a restroom stall.

That night I waited until the high school students turned back to face the front of the room, then excused myself. The thirty-yard walk from the classroom to the restroom was one I would never forget, and it was a walk I would make often.

I didn't want to face any more scrutiny from the high school students, so beginning that night, every Wednesday at about 7:05 p.m. I went to the restroom stall and just sat there. Sometimes I just sat and thought and sometimes I played a video game. I always waited as long as I could, hoping to miss the entire forty-five-minute group time, and then I would come out and meet the other thirteen-year-olds in our classroom for the second half of the youth service.

When I hid in the restroom stall, I felt safe.

NFL locker rooms are far different from restroom stalls, but some principles remain the same. The locker room is a place of constant interaction and communication, but believe it or not, insecurities run high. Music often booms from the speakers, and elite-level athletes argue with one another about a variety of things. In a place like a locker room, where you interact with your peers on a daily basis, you would think it would be impossible to hide.

It wasn't.

My rookie year was hard. I had been a committed Christian for most of my life, but I hadn't faced too much backlash for it, even in locker rooms. You see, in college, I always had guys around me who followed Jesus. We were a team, and more than that, we were a family, and we usually did everything together. We attended classes together, we went to parties together, and, of course, we pushed each other on the field. Suffice it to say that we sharpened one another.

The NFL was an entirely different atmosphere. Many of my peers and coaches weren't ready for committed Christians in this highly competitive league. I'm not sure I was ready for it either. Football is a competitive sport, and I am a competitive person. Whether it was a race or a drill in practice, I always wanted to come out on top. I thrived on the brutally competitive nature of the NFL, and of no surprise, many of my teammates did as well. My teammates and I would often get into altercations at practice, both physical and verbal, which was normal. What wasn't normal to many of my teammates was me. I was a competitor who was also a committed Christian. Many guys didn't know what to do with that, and it often put me in an awkward place.

If I ever got upset at a player or a coach, the guys would be all over me.

"Acho," they would say, "I thought you were a Christian. Christians aren't supposed to get mad! Was that a curse word I just heard?"

Many of those guys hadn't grown up around real Christians, followers of Christ who were free to be who God made them to be. I was a Christian who was free to get angry, and yes, like everyone else, I sinned from time to time. I knew who I was in Jesus, and that meant I was free to be competitive, free to glorify God with my gifts.

I believe we were created to compete and achieve, and I believe that competition can ultimately bring God glory. But at that point in my life, I didn't know how to respond to these questions or the ridicule that followed. So, instead, you can guess what I did. Yes, I hid. There was no restroom stall on the practice field, so I hid deep down within myself. I tried to hide my emotions. I tried to hide my anger. I didn't want to be a bad example for my teammates, and as a result, I didn't want them to see the *real* me. I was afraid of sharing who I really was inside, so I hid myself from everyone and put on a mask. Hiding like this wasn't healthy, and it didn't help me live out my fullest potential as a football player or as a child of God.

It wasn't until I started seeing a counselor and sharing my story and my scars that I began to get some real healing. He listened to a few of my stories and asked me a simple question: "What do you do when you get angry?"

My response was just as simple and direct: "I try not to get angry."

He wasn't buying it. After a little bit of back and forth and some careful, probing questions, we discovered the real answer: I hid. My counselor saw my hiding and drew me out into the light. You know what? God wants to do the same thing with every one of us. He's even doing it with me right now, as I write this book. In fact, I think he'd been seeking to draw me out into the open ever since those days in the youth group. I just hadn't allowed myself to step out of hiding.

That day with my counselor, though, as I faced the reality of how I hid from pain and people, I cried real, uncontrollable tears for the first time in a long time. I felt deeply ashamed. However, my tears weren't met with contempt or laughter; instead, they were met with a simple, refreshing response.

"Nice to see you, Sam," my counselor said. "Nice to see you. And by the way, get used to hearing that."

A few days later I found myself facing yet another decision to either hide or show my new teammates who I really was. After a long day at practice, a teammate saw a look on my face and asked what was going on. Usually, I would say that I was fine or tired. But this time, as a result of a lot of thought about what my counselor had recently told me, I determined then and there that this day would be different. I told my teammate what I was going through. I was completely honest with him. However, instead of being ridiculed, as I had previously feared, I was loved. He told me he had been there and recommended I keep letting it out. So I did, and the tears started to flow.

Another teammate noticed me crying and quickly

changed the locker room playlist. And wouldn't you know it, the songs he played were the exact same songs I had been listening to on my own the night before. Songs about God's love for me. Songs of freedom. We started to worship God right there in the locker room.

I had been tired of pretending and hiding, and the weight of God's whisper was too much to take. From the music that was being played on our locker room speakers to the song playing in my heart, God was working on me, reminding me over and over of his love for me. He started to show me that he was pleased with me, and that he wasn't ashamed of who I was.

"Nice to see you, Sam," my teammates said.

I stopped hiding and stepped into who I really was, and it blessed those around me.

Hiding isn't healthy. It hurts both the one who hides and whatever (or whoever) he or she is hiding from. I'm learning now to name my emotions: fear, anger, shame, joy, excitement. I'm also learning to be open and to be myself. I've heard it said that when you hide one emotion, you hide them all. You cannot choose which emotions you cut yourself off from. If you try to cut off fear, you'll cut off joy as well. It's the way we're wired. It's how we were created. So I'm learning not to hide my emotions anymore and to be myself in every circumstance. And the benefits, both on and off the football field, have been endless. I'm free. I'm me. And I'm a breath of fresh air to those around me.

**If you try to cut off fear, you'll cut off joy as well.**

Now don't get me wrong, I'm not perfect. I still wear

mismatched clothes on many Wednesday nights, I get upset easily, and I always want to win, many times to my detriment. But I'm me. And I'm not hiding anymore.

In 2018, four weeks into my eighth season as an NFL linebacker, I tore a pectoral muscle and my season was over. As soon as I heard the news from the doctor, I was devastated, and tears came to my eyes. My first reaction, honestly, was to find the nearest restroom stall. I actually started walking there so no one would see me cry. But since those days with my counselor, I had learned the importance of being *with* my emotions, so I made a different decision than my thirteen-year-old self would have. I allowed myself to be seen. I stopped in the hallway, a few yards short of the restroom, and cried. Right then and there. And I was seen by both my teammates and the staff of the Chicago Bears.

Much to my surprise, I wasn't judged. I wasn't condemned. I was loved. They sat with me. They mourned with me. They cried with me. They saw me, the real me, and that honesty was a breath of fresh air to the people around me. Their response was similar to others I'd gotten before: "Nice to see you, Sam. Nice to see you."

Locker rooms, like businesses and bars, hallways and homes, are easy places to find ways to hide. Instead of hiding in a restroom stall, though, people choose to hide within themselves and then put on masks in order to fit in. The reason I left that youth group so many years ago was the same reason I tried not to get angry in front of my

NFL teammates: I was afraid to be seen. I was afraid to be known. I was afraid to be me. Maybe you can relate to that feeling, but I'm here to tell you that hiding does not produce growth. In fact, it does the opposite; hiding stymies growth altogether. We create habits and make conscious or unconscious decisions to try to escape from pain, fear, and insecurity. But instead of escaping our emotions, our hiding compounds it all.

Hiding in the restroom stall is never the answer. Neither is hiding within yourself. We are meant to be seen, known, and loved. We are created by a Master Craftsman who wants us to show the world who we are. He wants us to shine. That is why Jesus tells us:

> You are the light of the world. A town built on a hill cannot be hidden. Neither do people light a lamp and put it under a bowl. Instead they put it on its stand, and it gives light to everyone in the house. In the same way, let your light shine before others, that they may see your good deeds and glorify your Father in heaven. (Matt. 5:14–16)

We serve a God who loves us. Don't hide. Don't be ashamed. Show people who you are. Be you. God gets the glory when you do because he created you with unique gifts, experiences, hopes, and dreams. And he wants you to share them with the world. So let your light shine.

chapter two

# CHILLIN' WITH
# THE PRESIDENT

The NFL is an interesting place. There are different calibers of players on different calibers of teams. Some are rookies. Some are veterans. Some are starters. Some are backups. Some are millionaires. Some are barely making ends meet. I was a combination of all of these.

A year after my rookie season, in spring 2012, I had earned a starting spot. I wasn't a millionaire, but I had been drafted in the fourth round and had received a large enough contract to make an upgrade from my college-plus checking account. I'll never forget the look on the teller's face when I attempted to deposit my six-figure signing bonus into my account, which until then had a balance in the hundreds of dollars, not the hundreds of thousands. Let's just say she was a little bit surprised.

Now that my rookie year was over, I was trying to find

my place. And the best way I saw to do that was by building a relationship with the biggest name on our team and in the NFL: Larry Fitzgerald.

Fitz, as his teammates liked to call him, was the Man. He was arguably the best wide receiver in the NFL and easily the highest-paid guy on our team. Rookies generally didn't talk to Fitz. Second-year players didn't either. So my approach had to be different.

Since showing up for my first training camp with the Arizona Cardinals, the number of calls I got asking about Fitz seemed endless.

"What kind of guy is he?" they asked. "Is he a believer? He called my Young Life group once. Is he as cool in real life as he seems on TV?"

"He's pretty cool," I replied. "He's an amazing player with an amazing work ethic." I would go on and on about his practice habits and his acrobatic one-handed catches. But when they asked about his character, I simply lied.

You see, though by then I had played with Larry for an entire season, I had yet to actually *speak* to him. His locker was on the other side of the locker room from mine, and as a rookie, I was scared to try to start a conversation with him. In my mind, he was in a different category than me, on a different level.

So when my friends asked me about him, I pretended as much as I could, until finally I had to tell them the truth: I didn't know anything about my teammate.

My hesitancy to get to know Fitz reminds me of the story of Nicodemus in the Bible. Nicodemus was a Pharisee, and Pharisees were the Jewish leaders who knew all about the Scriptures and were referred to as Israel's teachers (John 3:10). They were set apart and supposedly different from the rest. However, they knew nothing about Jesus, just as I knew nothing about Larry.

But Nicodemus wanted to learn more about Jesus and was determined to approach him. Yet he still made it a point to wait until nighttime to start a conversation with Jesus so he wouldn't be seen. Nicodemus didn't want his peers to catch him conversing with this supposedly classless person.

It's interesting to see how Jesus interacted with Nicodemus, talking about faith and being born again. Their conversation in John 3 includes one of the most well-known verses in the Bible. Jesus reminded Nicodemus of God's love: "For God so loved the world that he gave his one and only Son, that whoever believes in him shall not perish but have eternal life" (v. 16).

God used Nicodemus, a man who was stepping out of his shell, a man who finally stopped hiding and pretending, to spread the most repeated verse in the Bible. That's amazing! I doubt Nicodemus even realized the significance of his being himself in that moment. He was likely afraid and hesitant to approach Jesus, but he did it anyway. And it brought hope to the entire world.

I also find interesting the examples of light Jesus used in his conversation with Nicodemus. In the verses that follow he shared:

For God did not send his Son into the world to condemn the world, but to save the world through him. Whoever believes in him is not condemned, but whoever does not believe stands condemned already because they have not believed in the name of God's one and only Son. This is the verdict: Light has come into the world, but people loved darkness instead of light because their deeds were evil. Everyone who does evil hates the light, and will not come into the light for fear that their deeds will be exposed. But whoever lives by the truth comes into the light, so that it may be seen plainly that what they have done has been done in the sight of God. (vv. 17–21)

I don't believe it's a coincidence that Jesus used these examples of light while talking to someone at night. Someone who was hiding. As Nicodemus learned, if we come to the light and show the world who we are, God just might use us to change the course of history.

After this conversation, Nicodemus was forever changed. At the end of Jesus' life, Nicodemus was one of the guys who requested to take Jesus' body and bury it. This is important. Upon first meeting Jesus, Nicodemus had approached him at night. Hiding. But after being himself and encountering Jesus, his approach totally changed. He came to Jesus in the light of day. Unashamed. At a time when no one else wanted to be associated with Jesus. He and one of Jesus' disciples requested the body, embalmed it with spices, and buried it in a brand-new tomb (John 19:38–40).

Not to be lost is the detail Scripture gives that Nicodemus brought seventy-five pounds of spices with him. *Seventy-five pounds!* The same guy who was afraid to be seen with Jesus in the daytime was now carrying a huge bag of spices to prepare the body for burial *and* requesting permission to bury his body according to Jewish custom. Nicodemus had been changed. He had seen the light. He was himself, and he saw the freedom that came with it.

Being you is not only for the benefit of others. It's for you as well. *Being you changes you.* Better yet, it reveals the parts about you that you may not even know you have.

Nicodemus was not alone that day when he asked to bury Jesus. With him was a man named Joseph from the town of Arimathea. Joseph was hiding too. The Bible says that Joseph was a disciple of Jesus, "but secretly because he feared the Jewish leaders" (v. 38). Don't forget that Nicodemus was one of these Jewish leaders whom Joseph feared. Now the two men were side by side caring for Jesus' body. I don't think it's a coincidence that God chose Nicodemus to accompany Joseph in the burial of Jesus. Nicodemus was once afraid too. But God had bigger plans for him. Now he was free from fear and, without even knowing it, able to help free others.

> Being you is not only for the benefit of others. It's for you as well.

Fear can be crippling, yet Nicodemus put his fear aside and got to know Jesus. And in doing so he was forever changed. As was Joseph from Arimathea. As were you and I. What I learned from this story is that being you serves more purposes than you can imagine. Being you helps you and those around you and those you may never even meet. Being you pays big.

✄

Now it was time for me to be me. Though I was afraid, one of my friends encouraged me to talk to Larry. So I did. I set aside my fear and struck up a conversation.

One thing about me is that I notice things. More specifically, I notice things about *people*. One thing I noticed in my time around Fitz was that he cared about what people thought of him. He seemed interested in the image he portrayed. So when I started my first conversation with him, I said something I knew would get his attention.

"Fitz," I began, "a few of my friends from college have been calling me and asking about you. They ask about your character and why it is that you do the good deeds that you do."

I paused, not sure if I had overstepped my boundaries.

"Well," he said, "what do you tell them?"

I responded as honestly as I knew how. "I tell them I don't know anything about you and I have no idea what kind of guy you are or why it is you do what you do."

He was shocked. Surprised that I, like most people, didn't just lie to my friends and protect both his and my image. He was also probably shocked I told him the truth. Most people lie. We pretend to protect our reputations. We hide, afraid of what will happen if we're seen, if we're authentic. Thanks to some good friends, I decided not to hide anymore. I was honest with my superstar teammate, and it gave him a sense of refreshment he probably hadn't experienced in a while. He was relieved that someone around him was finally being real. And that feeling, that openness and taking off my mask, led to a surprising response, one I will never forget.

He paused, looked right at me, and said, "Well, how about you get to know me?"

That conversation led to a relationship that has lasted for years, even after I stopped playing for the Cardinals. I learned everything I could about Fitz. I learned what drove him to be the best and what separated him from others. I learned about his likes and dislikes, his passions and his pain points. He invited me to his house often. We would talk, hang out, and play chess. We became friends. One thing I realized about playing in the NFL is that professional athletes have a lot of people around them: coaches, critics, fans, and family. But the one thing many NFL players don't have is friends. Real friends. People who are for them. People who love them regardless of their on-field performance.

God doesn't care about our performance. He cares about us. The sooner we get to know that, the freer we become. I think that's what my friend Jerry Price wanted me to know the whole time. Why he told me to get to know Jesus. Because then I would get to know love. I would have a friend.

People need friends in their lives, so I became that for Fitz. And it changed everything. We spent time together and built trust between us. I told him about my Nigerian background, my belief in Jesus, my social stances, and my political views. I was me. People often fear that if they show their true selves, they will be judged or cast out. But I found the opposite is true. I showed Fitz exactly who I was: a loving, intelligent NFL player who cares about society and the people around him. I dropped my mask.

I had always thought that if people found out I was good at chess or was getting my master's degree in the off-season, they would think I wasn't fit for the league or NFL material. Boy, was I wrong. I revealed myself, my full self, to the biggest, baddest guy on our team. And it paid off.

I think this is what Nicodemus felt after being himself with Jesus. He saw he wasn't judged but loved. And it changed everything. Masks keep us hidden. They repress things about us that make us unique. We were meant to be seen and known, not masked and hidden. Masks are suffocating too. We need to breathe.

You were designed by God with a purpose, not by accident. Believe that truth. Live that truth. Being you pays off big. Trust me.

After a few months of Fitz and me getting to know each other in the off-season, the actual season began. NFL seasons can be brutal. Long days, late nights, busy weekends. I was going into my second year and was trying to solidify myself as a starter. I was working as hard as I could each week to prepare for our games on Sunday. Watching film, sitting in cold tubs, and meeting with coaches after practice to make sure I was primed to perform. A typical workday would start around 7:00 a.m. and finish around 5:30 or 6:00 p.m. I had a routine, and it was working for me. Until an unexpected offer changed everything.

I received a text from Fitz late one Tuesday night, asking about my after-practice plans for Wednesday. Wednesdays were our hardest day of practice: full pads, long meetings, and extra workouts. In the past I would have tried to impress him by sounding busy to show him I was focused and ready for the game. But this time was different. I was learning to be me. I reread the text before responding and noticed something interesting. His text seemed like more of an invitation than an inquiry. Fitz trusted me. He never seemed to be too worried about my preparation for Sunday's game. So instead of acting too busy, I was honest.

"I'm chillin', bro. What's up?"

He replied, "I've got a friend I would like you to meet. Be ready by 6:00 p.m. Dress to impress."

I wondered who his friend was and eagerly anticipated the next day's activities. I woke up early in the morning and rushed to practice, anxiously waiting for it to end. About halfway through, I asked Fitz who I was going to be meeting.

"Just wait and see," he replied.

A few hours later, I was in a room behind a room that was behind a room in a hotel, at a table with Fitz's friend: former president Bill Clinton. He and Fitz had worked on projects together with the Starkey Hearing Foundation, which provides hearing aids to people in underdeveloped countries, including many in Africa.

Fitz had remembered the conversations we had about my time in Nigeria doing medical mission work. He had heard me talk about my passion for Nigeria and my love for its people. President Clinton was in Phoenix for a speaking engagement, and Fitz thought we should meet.

Being me opened a door I never could have expected. Fear tries to inhibit us. It keeps us from living the life God intends for us, a life meant for refreshing people. Being me refreshed one of my teammates who was desperately seeking it. And being me benefitted me as well.

During our two-hour talk, I had a chance to share my passion for Africa with the former president. I told him about my family and our annual trips there to serve the needy. I talked and talked and talked. I thought the night couldn't get any more interesting, until the door to the room opened. I turned around, and much to my surprise, another president walked in: George W. Bush.

I was truly shocked. I had no idea there would be two former presidents at this event.

Our conversation continued, and I left that night blown away.

I learned President Bush is a University of Texas fan, and he had seen me play in college. We talked about the national championship game he had attended and the Dallas-area high school I attended. As it turned out, he was a next-door neighbor with one of my former classmates. We talked until it was time for the presidents to go on stage to speak. After they left, I just sat there, feeling a little stunned by what had just happened.

Things would get even better. Both presidents gave me a shout-out during their presentation. They talked about my family's mission work and my time at Texas. I had no idea they knew, cared, or remembered who I was. But they did. I was me, and it paid off big.

Proverbs 18:16 says, "A man's gift makes room for him

and brings him before the great" (ESV). I experienced this truth firsthand.

Use your gift. No matter what it is. Your courage, your experience, your family's experience, your inexperience. Be you. Stop hiding. Stop pretending. Take off the mask. It is time to be seen. It is time to be known. It's time to be that breath of fresh air that God breathed into you. God loves you. He is for you. He sees you and is pleased with you. Go start a conversation. Get to know another person. Use your gift, and it will put you in the presence of the great. Maybe even presidents.

## chapter three

# FREE CHIPOTLE

Sometimes we don't want to be seen. Being seen involves questions and conversations we're not always ready for. I ran into this after my second year with the Arizona Cardinals. I had just finished a tough workout and decided to stop by a Chipotle to grab a quick bite. But I hadn't showered. So my goal was to get in, get out, and get moving. Little did I know, God had different plans.

As this particular Chipotle was only about five minutes from my house, I went there often. After practices. With friends. Even with teammates. This day's visit seemed no different from any other—until it wasn't.

As I learned in 2 Peter 3:8, God supersedes time. He is infinite and time does not limit him. There are certain points in life when he puts you in the right place at the right time. You just need to make sure you're paying attention. I believe God is constantly trying to slow us down and remind us to walk with him, trust him, allow him to plan our day instead of planning it ourselves. And every so often, God will sidetrack us and remind us of his goodness. This day at Chipotle happened to be one of those days for me.

~

"Can I get a bowl, please?" I began, looking down, hoping to not make eye contact with the server. "Black beans, brown rice, double chicken," I continued.

The process was going smoothly. By avoiding eye contact I was expediting the ordering process.

I had become an expert at avoiding conversations. It was a mask I learned to put on. Don't get me wrong, I love people. I love learning about people, listening to their stories, and making sure they feel loved. But as a professional athlete, it seemed like you were not *supposed* to love people. At least not at an intimate level. Instead, you were supposed to let them love you. Early in my career my teammates often teased me for spending too much time talking with fans and showing too much interest in their lives. So I learned to love my fans a little less and let them love me a little more.

The only issue was the me they loved wasn't really me. It was a persona I put on to meet people's expectations. I was supposed to be larger than life, but in reality I'm not. I was supposed to be fake. Hence I put on a mask of inaccessibility.

I wasn't supposed to care about the server at Chipotle, so I tried not to. But this mask wasn't comfortable to wear, and I wasn't being me when I wore it. Still, I wore it because

I was trying to fit in with what I thought was now expected of me.

I don't think God is pleased when we do this, however. James 2:1–5 gives us some stern words concerning those who show favoritism and treat some people differently from the way they do others:

> My dear brothers, you are believers in our glorious Lord Jesus Christ. So never think that some people are more important than others. Suppose someone comes into your church meeting wearing very nice clothes and a gold ring. At the same time a poor man comes in wearing old, dirty clothes. You show special attention to the one wearing nice clothes. You say, "Please, sit here in this good seat." But you say to the poor man, "Stand over there," or "Sit on the floor by my feet!" What are you doing? You are making some people more important than others. With evil thoughts you are deciding which person is better.
>
> Listen, my dear brothers! God chose the poor in the world to be rich with faith. He chose them to receive the kingdom God promised to people who love him. (ICB)

God says to love others the way you love yourself and not to show favoritism. He says there's no place for it in his kingdom. He calls those thoughts *evil*.

Considering the way I was trying to hide from the Chipotle server, I clearly hadn't been paying too much attention to that passage.

I continued with my order until finally I was caught.

"Are you from Texas?" the server asked. It was a simple question.

I gave a brief one-word answer and moved on. "Yup. Guacamole, salsa, and sour cream, please." I hoped he wouldn't ask any more questions. But it didn't work.

"Awesome," he replied. "Did you play football there?"

I made sure to keep all my responses short. "I did." And then I continued with my order, hoping he would get the point. He didn't.

"That's awesome!" he said. "What do you do now?"

This was the one question I was doing my best to avoid. I was sweaty, smelly, and not put together. I did not want to be seen. But the problem with masks is that they're hard to maintain. You have to decide when to take them off and when to put them on. I didn't want to take mine off, but I also didn't want to lie, knowing he might already have an idea of who I was. So I responded to his question as honestly as I could and finished my order.

"I play for the Cardinals. Chips and salsa, please." I was ready for the check. Ready to get out of there. The problem was, he wasn't done.

"Wait, are you Sam Acho?!" he exclaimed.

"Yeah," I sighed, frustrated at his persistence and disappointed I had been noticed, sweat stains and all. No jersey, no pads, no million-dollar smile. Just me. I wasn't sure what was coming next. I expected him to ask for a picture or an autograph, so I prepared myself. But he did the last thing I expected. He built me up.

He called out, "Guys, this is Sam Acho! He plays for the Cardinals!" Then he continued, "Hey, dude, I see you in here all the time, and I didn't know you were a professional athlete. You're always nice to the employees here, and we really appreciate that. We have this thing called a Chipotle card. It gives you free Chipotle for a year."

I was floored. He said the staff would like to nominate me for the coveted card.

I was suddenly no longer in a rush. "Yes! Sure! What do you need from me?"

"Well, Sam," he said, "all we need is your number, and we can start the process."

At this point, being seen didn't matter. My mask was off. I was ready to give my cell phone number, my jersey number, even my social security number. I loved Chipotle, and this opportunity was too good to pass up.

Thankfully, all he needed was a cell phone number. He said he would pass it on to the regional marketing director.

I had hit the jackpot. I was a phone call away from having free Chipotle for a year. I figured the call would be easy enough: answer a few questions, sign an autograph or two, and talk about football. Boy, was I wrong. Once again, I had to decide whether I would be me or continue to hide.

❦

A few hours later I received a call from Kennedy Turner, the regional marketing director for Chipotle.

"Hey, Sam, hope you're well. Before we start, I've got a quick question for you. Are you a Christian?"

I didn't know how to answer that. I was without a doubt a follower of Jesus, but I'd never been asked that directly, especially when something I valued was on the line. At that moment I thought I understood a little better how Peter must have felt right before Jesus' death, when three times he was faced with the decision of whether to deny knowing Jesus.

After Jesus had been arrested and led to the high priest for questioning, Peter had followed at a discreet distance. But when he was identified as one who had been "with Jesus of Galilee" (Matt. 26:69), he denied it, afraid of what would happen to him.

Admittedly, my situation was on a slightly smaller scale. Peter was deciding between life and death; my decision revolved around free food. But from what I understood about the corporate world, being affiliated with Jesus was taboo, and it seemed as if my dreams of free burritos hinged on my response.

After a few moments, I replied, "Yes, I am. I'm a follower of Jesus."

I wish my response had been bolder or more confident, but it wasn't. Sometimes you don't know how you'll respond to a situation until you're in it. I always thought I was unashamed of my relationship with Jesus, but when something as trivial as free food was on the line, I hesitated.

"Interesting," he responded. "I went on your Twitter page and read something about your faith in Jesus, and it made me stop."

I was done. Exposed and seen again. I had lost my opportunity for free Chipotle. *Hopefully God is happy*, I thought. I expected the conversation to be over, but it wasn't.

Kennedy continued, "I stopped because I'm a follower

of Jesus as well. I know it's hard in my line of work to openly talk about my faith in Christ. It must be hard for you as well. I would love to grab lunch with you and talk more."

So we did. We met up the following week and had a conversation about faith in the workplace, soccer, and free Chipotle. A few months later I received the coveted card and enjoyed using it for a year. Actually, many years. Kennedy renewed the card for me many times. It was a great experience. But more than the food, I gained a friend.

Kennedy had young kids and a new marriage. I was on the verge of proposing to my soon-to-be wife and had a strong desire to be a father as well. I learned a lot from Kennedy. I learned that being me really does pay off, and that I can be an encouragement to others even when I try not to.

☙

Being you can be hard. But it doesn't have to be. The quicker we stop pretending, the quicker we receive the benefits God has in mind for us. Psalm 37:4 says, "Take delight in the LORD, and he will give you the desires of your heart." God is delighted when we love the people around us and talk about him, when we're proud of our faith in him. But even when we are not, he still loves us. Just ask Peter.

After Jesus was raised from the dead and appeared to his disciples, he gave Peter an opportunity for redemption and allowed Peter to reaffirm his love for him. And Peter did. Three times. Jesus used Peter to begin what we now know as the church, despite Peter's doubts and failures.

God is a God who redeems broken situations and broken people.

At Chipotle I was trying to hide. What I didn't realize was that I had already been seen all the other times I had walked into that restaurant. I was me. And I was loved, even though I didn't realize it. The same goes for you. God sees you. He knew you while you were in your mother's womb. He has good plans for you. Remember that. Know that. Believe that. God has already seen your Twitter page too. You're marked with his blood. You are redeemed. You don't have to pretend anymore. You don't have to hide. Take off the mask and come sit at the table. Dine with Jesus.

◆

That Chipotle card was a blessing for me. And it was used to bless others. I would throw Chipotle parties for classmates, teammates, kids, and communities. I would gift Chipotle to total strangers. I even made friends with some of the workers whom I had tried to avoid in the past. I was me. God honored that. God wants that joy for all of us. He has good, good gifts that he wants us to have. And he wants us to bless other people with them. The sooner we take off our masks, the sooner we can enjoy God's gifts and share them with others.

**The sooner we take off our masks, the sooner we can enjoy God's gifts and share them with others.**

Free Chipotle wasn't meant only for me; it was meant for those around me. It was meant to be a blessing to others. You are too. Let yourself be seen. Sweat stains and all. You are loved. You are known. You are his. Come and enjoy the meal.

## chapter four

# MOVIES FOR DAYS

New people and new places evoke new emotions. I had just graduated from college and had reached my dream: being drafted by an NFL team. The only problem was, I wasn't allowed to play. At the time, there was a lockout in effect, which meant that the teams were allowed to draft new players, but those players were not allowed to attend any official practices.

I'll never forget the call I received on draft day from team president Michael Bidwill: "Congratulations, Sam! You're an Arizona Cardinal!"

I was beyond excited. I had reached my goal, and this call was only the beginning. I was determined to set the league on fire. God had answered my prayers, and I was ready to do everything in my power to make an immediate impression with my new employer.

In my excitement, I asked what I should do next. It was

an easy question, but easy questions, as I soon found out, don't always have easy answers.

"Well," Mr. Bidwill replied, "I'm not sure where you're at right now, but wherever you are, stay there. You're not permitted to come to our practice facility until this lockout issue is resolved."

The lockout was a labor dispute between the players and the team owners. Labor disputes are nothing new, but this one was a little different. The 2009 financial crisis had taken a toll on everyone, including the NFL owners. And they weren't too excited about the prospect of moving forward with the labor deal that was in place. They wanted a better deal and were willing to sacrifice a season or two to get it.

But I wasn't. I got off the phone with mixed emotions. I was still excited about being drafted, but I was unsure where I was supposed to go from here. I'm a doer, and since God had answered my prayers so clearly and directly, I was ready to go. Full steam ahead! No owner or lockout was going to stop that. One way or another I was on my way to Arizona. I just needed to figure out how.

The how turned out to be easy. Social media had taken off, and my older sister had created a Twitter account for me a few weeks earlier. Now was the time to use it. The problem was, I didn't know anyone on the team. What a lot of people didn't realize was that I never really watched professional football. In college we had practices on Sundays, and I had classes on Mondays. I figured I could always catch the game highlights on ESPN if needed. Now that these guys were my teammates, I had a lot of learning to do.

My research started on Twitter. I searched for guys on the Cardinals' roster who seemed normal. The search started and stopped with Calais Campbell. Calais is a gentle giant. He's six feet, eight inches tall and a solid three hundred pounds. None of those numbers are normal per se, but Calais is an amazing human being. He's got the biggest smile known to man, and he's one of the nicest guys I know. I reached out to him on Twitter and asked if there was a good place to train in Arizona while I waited for the lockout to end. He gave me directions to his training facility in Scottsdale. I asked if I could train with him, and he obliged.

A few days later I showed up at the gym, but Calais was nowhere to be found. Pretty soon someone asked me if I was one of the Cardinals players. Technically I was, so I said yes. He directed me to a workout area where the players were getting ready to begin their lift.

One thing I had learned over the years was to fake it, to pretend, to act like I belonged. Even when I didn't know who I was, I always had a pretty good idea of who I was expected to be. In school I was a star athlete, at home I was a peacemaker, at church I was the pastor's son. Putting on all these masks was effortless for me. And they worked too. People got what they expected and seemed happy. But faking it can only get you in the door. Being who God made you is what keeps you there.

**Faking it can only get you in the door. Being who God made you is what keeps you there.**

I'm reminded of Moses, a Hebrew boy who had been pretending. He was adopted as a baby into an Egyptian family that owned Hebrew slaves. He acted Egyptian, but he looked like a Hebrew. His true calling would be to free the Hebrew slaves, but pretending got him in the door.

My pretending got me in the door that day at the gym. The only problem was, now that I was in, I was going to be caught. I was in a workout with half a dozen Cardinals players, and none of the guys knew who I was.

By the grace of God, one of my new teammates, Adrian Wilson, took me under his wing. Adrian is a rock-solid, six-foot-three, 235-pound man of steel. People were legitimately scared of him, both his teammates and his opponents. Still, he and I became friends because I showed him the real me, and I saw the real him as well. A-Dub, as we called him, had his own masks, too, but the primary one was of a tough guy. He had a heart for kids. I'll never forget the day he invited me to his house to teach me the playbook. He had three young kids at the time, and I caught him humming the theme song of one of the kids' TV shows. The thing is, A-Dub had a reputation for never smiling. So hearing him sing these songs and unknowingly let his guard down opened the door for me. He showed me he was human and that he loves kids, just like me.

I still don't know if A-Dub knows what he did for me that day, but I'll never forget it. Of course, he made me promise not to tell anyone, a promise I kept for years—well, up to now. I think he was working through some insecurities too. But after that night at his house, he had my allegiance. Not only did he teach me the plays, but he also taught me how to be me. How to be real. How to let my guard down and have balance. That day, when I saw behind the mask of one of my teammates, I learned the freedom that comes from being me.

My arrival in Scottsdale wasn't the only time pretending got me through the door. A year or so later I was at a Phoenix Suns game with my friend Max, who provided the tickets. I didn't go to many sporting events when I was growing up, so I was excited about this new experience. But the Suns were getting blown out, so toward the end of the third quarter after most of the fans had left, Max and I decided to find better seats. We found a reasonable spot: section 105, row K, seats 1 and 2. We propped our feet up to enjoy the rest of the game. But things soon changed.

During a time-out, the PA announcer said, "Suns fans, it's time for your giveaway! And for this round, the lucky winners will be receiving free tickets to a prescreening of Marvel's *Avengers!*"

My ears perked up. Although I was making good money in the NFL, free is free. Plus the movie hadn't been released yet. I pulled out my ticket and eagerly awaited the announcement.

"Congratulations to those fans sitting in section 104, row J, seats 1 through 14. You win! Show your ticket stub at the exit and collect your prize."

*Must be nice*, I thought, looking at my ticket stub for section 400. Then, all of a sudden, I heard shouts of excitement.

I looked to my left and realized the winners were sitting right next to us. Right then and there I decided I had to find a way to get hold of those tickets.

One thing about me is that I'm great with people, so I struck up a conversation with the two guys to my left, who had won the prize, and put my people skills and my business skills to use. After about three minutes we agreed to a trade: two beers for two tickets.

With my golden tickets now in hand, I figured going to the movie would be a breeze. Boy, was I wrong.

On the day of the screening, my buddy Max and I showed up about an hour early at the theater in Glendale. We knew the place would be packed, but when we arrived, the line was literally out the door. We waited and waited and waited. After a while we overheard a couple in front of us talking about how they might not be able to watch the movie. The theater capacity was around 350 people, and we were waiting behind at least 400 to 500 ticket holders. Our chances of seeing the movie were slim to none. But we hadn't driven all the way to Glendale to be denied, so we came up with a plan.

"Follow me," Max said. "Don't say a word. Just look important."

After playing in the NFL for almost a year, I had learned to play that role well. I knew how to pretend. In fact, most people are good at this. We watch and we imitate. We have been doing that since we were children, so it should come as no surprise that we do the same as adults. As I learned that day at the Arizona gym, and again at the theater in Glendale, imitating may get you in the door, but being you will open doors you never imagined.

Max and I walked straight to the front of the line, and Max approached a woman who was monitoring the ticket taking and said, "Excuse me, can I speak with a manager, please? I've got an Arizona Cardinals player here, and he's really upset that he has to wait in this extremely long line. Something needs to be done immediately."

**Imitating may get you in the door, but being you will open doors you never imagined.**

I almost burst out laughing. I wasn't upset about anything. I was mostly shocked that my friend would be so bold.

"Are you his agent?" she asked.

"Yes, I am. And I need to speak with your manager as soon as possible."

Max was not my agent, but he was that night. A few moments later, Regina, the regional director for Marvel promotions, came up to us. She was there to ensure the prescreening went well.

"I am so sorry, Mr. Acho," she began, looking at me in the eye.

I was no longer finding all of this as funny as it seemed a few minutes before. Rather, I was feeling extremely uncomfortable in front of the long line of people I had cut ahead of. At this point I was ready to go back and stand in line like everyone else. I figured we had to accept the fact that we weren't going to see the movie. But then Regina said something that really surprised me.

"I'm sorry I didn't have your name on the list," she said. "We sent an email to the community relations director at the Cardinals about this event but never heard back. I've been trying to get ahold of someone on the team so we can invite them to some of our screenings or maybe even do some type of partnership with them. Would you mind being our contact person?"

Dreams really *do* come true. I love people. I love bringing people together around good causes. And I love free stuff. This relationship was the perfect opportunity for someone like me. Not only did Regina give us great seats that day, but she also held our phones in her purse since we weren't allowed to bring them into the theater, and she didn't want to make us go back to the car.

Regina and I talked before and after the movie. I thanked her for her kindness and for her interest in partnering with the team. And I became the unofficial movie guy for the Arizona Cardinals. My teammates loved it, and I was using the gifts God gave me. We watched movies as a team, with fans, and even with firefighters. We also watched movies with kids from tough neighborhoods who rarely get opportunities to see movies in a theater, let alone with a group of professional athletes. We threw Chipotle parties for them too. (Those were fun, but they were a logistical nightmare!)

What I learned that day is that even when we pretend, God sees us, knows us, and puts us exactly where we need to be when we need to be there.

Regina saw the real me. A-Dub did as well. I'm still friends with both of them to this day. However, there's no pretending anymore. Be you. When you are, others will benefit.

## chapter five

# BARGAINING WITH BILLIONAIRES

"You wanna fly back with me?" he asked, as if he were giving me a lift down the road. But all that was going through my mind was the return ticket I had with Delta.

"I'll pass," I responded.

"Well, next time we're both in Dallas, we should fly together. Shoot, we'll just have Jerry take us on *his* jet!" he said with a smile.

He was Clark Hunt, the owner of the Kansas City Chiefs, an NFL franchise valued at $2 billion. Jerry, of course, was Jerry Jones, whose $5.5 billion Dallas Cowboys were, according to *Forbes* magazine, the most valuable sports franchise in the world.

Clark and I had a few things in common. We both went to St. Mark's School of Texas, a small private school in the

Dallas area. Their football field is actually named after his father. But our commonalities stopped there.

Jerry and I had even less in common. If there were a list of words to describe Jerry Jones, *compassionate* would not be one of them. Yet here I was, sitting at the bargaining table with Clark Hunt, Jerry Jones, and five other NFL team owners, trying to negotiate a new collective bargaining agreement.

Our first meeting involved seven players, seven owners, and a few lawyers on each side. I didn't know what to expect, but one thing I did know, like that night I saw *The Avengers*, was how to *act* important. So that's how I began.

One by one, each of the seven owners, plus Commissioner Roger Goodell, shook my hand and introduced himself. I made sure not to smile. One thing that gives me away is my smile. It welcomes people and makes them feel loved. A smile is the kind of human warmness that can't be faked. I did not want to smile this day. My plan was to look as stern as possible. Some would call this a poker face. I convinced myself these billionaire owners were jerks who cared nothing about people, especially the players who sustained the game they profited greatly from. So I mustered up my best poker face and prepared for war.

But 2 Corinthians 5:17 says, "Therefore, if anyone is in Christ, he is a new creation" (NKJV). This means that being you involves growth. And right there at the negotiating table, God was in the process of changing me. He was in the process of showing me who I was. He planned on helping me overcome my fears and use the gifts he had given me for his good. And this day, that gift would be my voice.

I had heard about some of Jerry Jones's tactics. He used

enticing dialogue and had an ability to captivate a room. I was determined not to be impressed. But the more I sat in that room, the more I realized something: billionaires are people too. They have gifts just like me. They have struggles as well. No matter their net worth.

I see people. God made me unique in that way. I love people too. Another thing that makes me unique is my ability to speak. God gives me ideas and words to say that cut through the pain and get to the point. He also made me sensitive. People have said I'm *too* sensitive, but God thinks different. God gave me a special kind of sensitivity that can feel what people are going through and empathize with them. And that day, at the bargaining table, God combined my sensitivity with tact and opportunity. In the past, I would have sat quietly and said nothing, too afraid to speak up. But I've been scarred too many times not to use my voice for good.

❧

There's a place in Scripture where Paul reminded his friends in Rome about the power of using their voices. He reminded them of the words Moses told God's chosen people as he was leading them out of slavery: "The word is near you, in your mouth and in your heart" (Rom. 10:8 NKJV). One thing about me is that God's words have always been near me, in my mouth and in my heart. The problem was, I usually *kept* them there. I was always afraid to share them. But as Paul said: "Faith comes by hearing" (v. 17 NKJV). And it was time for me to speak so others could hear.

Jerry Jones had just said he wanted to get a deal done as soon as possible, and he would do whatever it took to get it. He also threatened to lock out the players and not pay them a dime if they did not comply with *his* terms.

I had listened long enough. It was time to speak. To speak truth to power. I cleared my throat and set my words free. I knew I had to say something to get his attention, so I decided to start by saying something similar to how I began my first conversation with Larry Fitzgerald.

"Billionaires don't become billionaires by being fair," I said.

I saw Jerry's ears perk up.

"But we have an opportunity to change the narrative. To be partners. To be an example for the world to see. Equity and fairness," I said. "That's what matters."

With that the first part of our meeting concluded. I had done it. I had taken off my mask. And I felt the freedom that came with it. It was like a cool, refreshing breeze; like a cup of cold water to a dry, parched mouth. I was me. And many people benefitted from it. I took off the mask and was no longer afraid.

And that smile I tried not to use? God had plans for that too.

❧

Have you ever heard an exceptional singer? Seen a natural-born dancer move? A soccer player bring a ball to life? There's something majestic about it all.

I was at a young adult gathering in Phoenix with about

eight hundred people. I was talking to some friends when the music began. All of a sudden everything stopped, and my ears perked up as if I heard the voice of an angel. I was sitting in the back so I couldn't see the stage, but I could hear the voice.

I came back two weeks later and heard the voice again. This time I had to find out who this person was, and that's how I met Dianne. I told her how much her voice blessed me and even asked her to sing at my wedding. I was amazed.

Being you will do that. It will blow people away. Maybe not because you have an angelic voice or a million-dollar smile or skills with a leather ball. Maybe it's your kindness. Maybe it's your tact. Maybe it's your simplicity. God made us all different. He knitted us in our mothers' wombs. God is creative. And he creates people in ways that bring him glory. Dianne's voice did that for me.

And my smile did that for an NFL owner.

Before the next meeting began, I went to the restroom for a quick break. I had no need to use the facilities. I just felt a prompting to go there. Sometimes such things happen. I'll feel as if I'm supposed to do something or go somewhere. It's not a loud voice but more of a leading. In those moments, I slow down and listen.

When I entered the restroom, I saw someone who had been at the prior meeting. He was one of the league's most prominent owners. On the one hand, he was the definition of success. He ran a successful business and a successful team, and he had boatloads of money in the bank. On the other hand, he was broken. He had just been caught up in a scandal, and his case was all over the news. He was broken. He was hurting. He was human.

I wasn't sure what I was supposed to do. In my heart I wanted to condemn him. I wanted people to see him, judge him, make him feel like a sinner. *How often do billionaires get caught in their sin? How often do they actually have to pay a penalty?* I thought to myself. I wanted him to pay the price that regular people would have to pay, and then maybe he would better understand what players go through. But after having seen him interact with another member of the executive committee earlier, I was gently reminded that grace is for everyone.

While he went about his business, he looked me in the eye and said, "You know, you have the greatest smile."

"Thanks," I said. "I get it from my mom."

And just like that the ice was broken. And my cover too. I had no idea how he had seen my smile during those meetings. I was doing my best to hide it. But for whatever reason, there we were, talking about it in, of all places, the restroom.

It's funny how God does things. He takes our greatest weaknesses and makes them our biggest strengths. He doesn't allow us to remain hidden. He loves us too much. Fifteen years prior, restroom stalls had been a place of hurt and hiding for me. In this moment, it was a place of freedom.

The owner and I continued to talk. He asked where my parents were from and inquired about my background. I told him about my dad who, as a pastor in Nigeria, was preaching from the top of a bus when some missionaries heard him. They were so impressed they invited him to minister to people in America. God opened a door with my dad and these missionaries. Now God was opening a door for me.

I could tell the owner was hurting. He talked about his issues with religion, and I listened. But one thing I've learned about Jesus is that he couldn't care less about religion. He wants relationship. So that's how I directed our conversation. When the owner asked about my faith and which religious sect I affiliated with, I told him about Jesus. About how I followed him and was trying my best to get to know him deeply. About how he's a loving and kind God. And about his forgiveness. I talked about how in most religions all that matters are your good deeds. But when you follow Jesus, all that matters is him. I talked about his grace, his forgiveness, and his seemingly irrational love.

I could tell the owner was listening. At that point, I knew I wasn't in that restroom by accident. We washed our hands and headed out the door. I told him the Bible story about a woman caught in adultery whom supposedly religious people were ready to condemn. But Jesus said to them, "Let any one of you who is without sin be the first to throw a stone at her" (John 8:7).

He knew the story, but he didn't know how it ended. I told him after all the accusers dropped their stones and walked away, Jesus told the woman, "Neither do I condemn you. Go now and leave your life of sin" (v. 11).

"I know the feeling," the owner responded, empathizing

with the prostitute who felt condemned by everyone around her.

"I do too," I said. "The only difference is that I realized I can ask Jesus for forgiveness. And he'll give it."

I felt proud of myself for telling this owner about the good news of Jesus. I was expecting some immaculate response, an amazing change, but there wasn't one. He simply said as we walked back to the bargaining table, "You have good parents."

I don't know what that conversation did for him. But one thing I do know is that God is in the business of redeeming broken situations. For me it was the restroom stall. He used my place of hiding and reshaped it into a place of healing. A place of forgiveness. Where is your restroom stall? What areas of life have you been avoiding? Allow God into your broken situations. Be you.

I had walked into these meetings with the mindset that the owners were the enemy. I saw them as manipulative, greedy, and evil. To say that the relationship between them and the players was contentious would be an understatement. It was us versus them. But Jesus desired something more. He wanted his followers to be different. He wanted to show us more of his character. He wanted us to be more like God. That's why he said:

> You have heard that it was said, "You shall love your neighbor and hate your enemy." But I say to you, Love

your enemies and pray for those who persecute you, so that you may be sons of your Father who is in heaven. For he makes his sun rise on the evil and on the good, and sends rain on the just and on the unjust. For if you love those who love you, what reward do you have? (Matt. 5:43–46 ESV)

A few months later, these enemies would become friends. I chose to pray for my enemies and to use the gifts God gave me. As we continued to negotiate, relationships were formed and bonds were built. The people I thought I would never be able to relate with became acquaintances. It took courage and it took obedience, but it was well worth it. God is calling you for more.

This wouldn't be the last time I had a chance to love my enemies. A few weeks later, after firing my agent, I was on the phone with general managers, head coaches, and scouts from teams all around the league.

Being your own agent is hard, even though I had previously thought it wasn't. As an agent, your job is to represent your player to a team that, at times, couldn't care less about him. Some of the people in the scouting department are just plain sour. Their job is to evaluate players' strengths and weaknesses on and off the field and then assign a dollar amount or a value to each player. Those doing the evaluations remain relatively anonymous during this process, and occasionally, with anonymity comes a sense of pride, power, and entitlement. An agent's job is to fight for their client and sometimes be the bearer of bad news.

I hoped I would be able to negotiate a better contract than my agent had done previously. And I wanted to show other players that they could do it too. I wanted to be different. What I learned was that negotiating wasn't the hard part; it was hearing all the negative reports from the so-called anonymous sources.

No one likes rejection, and I was getting tired of all the nos and the lack of responses. I knew I could still play, but I was a year older and coming off an injury—two factors that did not bode well for my reviews.

"He's not good enough anymore."

"He's lost a step."

"Ever since that injury, things haven't been the same."

"We're simply not interested."

I was hearing all of this through the grapevine and sometimes directly. I thought I could handle it, but it was hard. I talked with head coaches, general managers, assistant general managers, contract negotiators—all the decision makers. I wanted them to know I was available and excited about every opportunity to play. But they seemed not to care. Then a friend reminded me of who I am.

"Sam," he said, "you're highly relational. You love encouraging people. These people, the people at the top, are likely lacking in real relationships, lacking in true encouragement. So instead of trying to get something from them, why don't you try to give something to them. Encourage them. Pray for them. See where that takes you."

Whether or not my friend knew it at the time, he was encouraging me to put God to the test with a promise of Scripture: "Seek first the kingdom of God and his righteousness, and all these things will be added to you" (Matt. 6:33 ESV).

I had been focusing on getting what I wanted from these decision makers, when all along God was telling me to focus on giving and allow him to get for me what I was looking for.

So I changed perspective. Instead of calling teams for a job, I asked how I could pray for them. I had conversations with the people no one has access to, and I would pray for them. I would encourage them. I would remind them that their worth was so much more than their decisions. That there was a God in heaven who saw them and who knew them. Even after hearing them say no, I asked what they needed prayer for. Some said their families, some said balance in their lives, some said the health of their teams. But they all responded. They all wanted relationship. These men—the guys I would usually need a buffer to communicate with, the people I didn't understand—were just like me. I didn't learn that fact until I stopped trying to build my kingdom and instead started trying to build God's.

I now have relationships I never would have thought I needed. I now have people in my corner pulling for me, rooting for me, and praying for my success. Be you. But seek to be like Jesus. Love your enemies. Pray for those who curse you. Just as Jesus did.

Which enemies do you need to love? Which people do

you need to pray for? In what areas do you need to build God's kingdom and not your own? Freedom is right around the corner. Hope is just around the bend. Don't give up. Don't lose hope. You are needed. You are loved.

## chapter six

# BEAR DOWN

Where has life taken you? What paths or detours have you taken that seem like they don't make any sense? What do you do when bad news hits? Timing is everything. And everything happens for a reason. God is in the business of trading trouble for treasure. He will use your disappointments for good.

I'm reminded of the Bible story about Naomi and her daughter-in-law Ruth. Naomi was from the little town of Bethlehem. She married Elimelech and had two sons. Then a famine hit the country and there was no water in their homeland, so they traveled to an unfriendly territory to try and make ends meet. After being in this foreign land for a while, Elimelech died. Naomi's sons married women from the area, but then her sons also died. Naomi was stuck. She decided to go back home and told her daughters-in-law to do the same because she had nothing and didn't want to leave them with nothing too. One agreed, but one didn't.

Ruth decided to accompany her mother-in-law to a land that was foreign to her.

Ruth was loyal. She didn't pretend she had it all together. She was desperate, but she was unashamed too. She told Naomi, "Where you go I will go, and where you stay I will stay. Your people will be my people and your God my God. Where you die I will die, and there I will be buried" (Ruth 1:16–17). So Ruth and Naomi traveled to Bethlehem.

Sometimes your determination is what makes you different. It's a gift God gives you. It's how he wired you. Ruth was determined. She didn't care what anyone said or what they thought. She refused to take no for an answer. And thus, she became an integral part of the Bible story.

When they returned to Bethlehem, Naomi thought she would be ridiculed. She changed her name to Mara, which means "bitter," because she felt God had turned his back on her and was repaying her for some sin she had committed.

How many of us have felt this way? Distraught, depressed, dejected, hopeless.

This is a little of how I felt during my last year in Arizona. Everything seemed like it was going my way, but after suffering a broken leg the year before, things just weren't the same. My body, which I relied on heavily to be successful, wasn't working the way it used to.

It had gotten to a point where one of my coaches out of frustration said to me, "I hate watching you practice. You just do the same thing over and over again, and it doesn't work!"

I left feeling dejected. I wanted to perform better, but my body wasn't letting me.

Even one of my teammates noticed a difference. "Are you just scared to make a play?" he asked.

I wasn't scared; I was just unable to do it. Football was miserable that year. Although we were winning games, I hated going to practice. I knew that some of my coaches thought poorly of me as a player, and many of my teammates didn't hold me in high regard either. I was ready for a fresh start.

The next season I signed with the Chicago Bears, but something still wasn't right. My body was still in a good amount of pain. I didn't want to tell the coaches because I didn't want to give them an excuse to bench me, so I managed it. I coped and tried my best to be successful in my job, all the while wondering when things would get better.

It didn't make any sense to me. I didn't understand why I was still feeling the effects of a three-year-old injury. I didn't understand why, even though I felt as if I was performing better than my peers, I wasn't getting a fair chance. I also didn't understand why God chose to send me to Chicago of all places and not use me in the ways I thought I was supposed to be used. I wanted to be the star of the team. I wanted to be the captain. I wanted to be the hero. But God reminded me that he is the hero of the story. Not me. He also taught me that just because you're not the captain of the team, it doesn't mean you can't lead. Leaders come in different shapes and sizes and many different styles. So I decided to lead from behind.

That first year with the Bears, I wasn't playing much on defense, but the coaches gave me an opportunity on special teams. Special teams is a part of the game most people don't know about. If you're not a starter, you're relegated to special teams. Most of my teammates hated being on special teams, and I did too. Until God showed me it was not about me.

Colossians 3:23 says to do everything as if you're doing it for God and not for others. I decided to make the most of my opportunity as a special teams player. *If the coaches don't want to play me on defense,* I thought, *then I'll be the best special teams player they've ever seen.* And God made it work for me, both on and off the field.

On the field, I was chosen by my coaches as a Pro Bowl nominee for special teams. I also played well enough to earn another contract with the team the next year. But it was the off-the-field opportunities that left me speechless.

Although my job was important, God made it clear there were other things in the world that were more important. Once again I was reminded of Jesus' words in Matthew 6:33: "Seek first the kingdom of God and his righteousness, and all these things will be added to you" (ESV).

We had some big-name players on the team during my first year on the Bears, and then they all left. The coach was changing the culture and wanted to bring certain guys in who could implement it. There was something of a mass exodus. Our most well-known players—the ones most heavily involved in helping out the local community—were all gone, and there was a void that needed to be filled. I didn't have any plans, but I saw a need. So I filled it.

After spending a good amount of time serving the community, I noticed my perspective started to shift. I was thinking less and less about my desires and more and more about God's.

I think we often get caught up in the busyness of life. Society tells us that if we work hard enough, do well enough, try hard enough, or look pretty enough, then we will *be* enough. But there's a problem with that equation: we already *are* enough. Jesus showed us that he chose to die on the cross for us "while we were still sinners" (Rom. 5:8 NKJV). He didn't wait until we became perfect or mistake-free; Jesus died while we were in the midst of our sin because of his love. This truth is hard to comprehend. We ask ourselves, Who are we to be loved? Who are we to be favored? But who are we *not* to be loved? We are children of God. There's no denying it. So if you ever find yourself feeling unworthy or unloved, remember who your Dad is.

A few months later I found a letter in my locker after practice: "Congratulations, Sam, you have been nominated for the Walter Payton NFL Man of the Year Award. This award recognizes your work to help make the community around you better."

I was stunned. I thought this award was reserved for big-name players, like the guys who had been let go earlier. I also felt honored because the award was named after one of the best Chicago Bears players of all time, and I was playing for the Bears. I was also surprised because of what else was written on the letter: "As an added benefit to

> Society tells us that if we work hard enough . . . then we will *be* enough. But . . . we already *are* enough.

your hard work, we will be donating $50,000 to the charity of your choosing." I was confused. In years past, nominees for the award were granted $5,000 to their charity and the winner would receive $50,000.

Well, this year, my first year to be nominated, the committee had received a big-time sponsor, and that sponsor wanted to amplify the impact of the work the players were doing. Nominees now received $50,000 for their charity, with the winner receiving $500,000. And that amplification couldn't have come at a better time.

❧

My parents traveled every year to Nigeria and brought free medical care to people in need. They had seen a need for hurting people, so they decided to do something about it. They gathered thirty or so friends who had hearts to help the hurting as well. These friends came from different backgrounds. Some were doctors, some were singers, and some were students. This group of medical professionals and missionaries would spend two weeks of their summer serving the needy. The trips were going well, but my dad felt as if God was calling us for more. Calling us to build something. My dad is a dreamer and a builder. His desire was to see an entire community, an entire country, changed. Sometimes being you is bigger than you.

God gave my dad a dream of building a state-of-the-art medical facility in rural Nigeria. This was a part of the world where people died from dirty water and dysentery, insect bites and infections, and where cataracts, hernias, and skin lesions ran rampant. There was no electricity, no running water, and very little hope. It included the village where my grandfather had grown up. God gave my dad a vision, but we had no idea how he was going to accomplish it. And then I learned I had been nominated for the Payton Award.

That $50,000 went a long way toward getting the Living Hope Medical Center off the ground. Once people saw that it was being built, they decided to chip in and try to help finish it. Yet a year later we were still a bit short. Then I was nominated again. And with that additional $50,000, the Living Hope Medical Center was completed.

Your story is about more than just you. You may never understand why you suffered calamity or a breakup or the loss of a loved one, but God does. He has a purpose for your pain. He isn't wasting your situation. It might be hard, and you may not understand what is going on in the process, but be you. People are depending on it.

God is in the business of trading trouble for treasure. My first two seasons in Chicago were rough from a physical, spiritual, and emotional standpoint, but God was up to something much, much bigger than me. He was using me and my situation for his glory. All I had to do was stay the course.

Naomi's story wasn't much different. After she changed her name to Bitter, God gave her a sliver of hope. Ruth 2:1–3 says:

Now there was a rich man living in Bethlehem whose name was Boaz. Boaz was one of Naomi's close relatives from Elimelech's family.

One day Ruth, the woman from Moab, said to Naomi, "Let me go to the fields. Maybe someone will be kind and let me gather the grain he leaves in his field."

Naomi said, "Go, my daughter."

So Ruth went to the fields. She followed the workers who were cutting the grain. And she gathered the grain that they had left. It just so happened that the field belonged to Boaz. He was a close relative from Elimelech's family." (ICB)

Boaz was generous to both Ruth and Naomi. After seeing and hearing about the kindness and character of Ruth, he made sure she and Naomi were well taken care of. He would give her extra food and make sure his servants treated her with kindness and respect. But God had bigger plans for both of them. When Naomi learned that Ruth was gathering from Boaz's field, she had an idea. She remembered a custom that a close relative could marry a widow without children so she could have children. And Boaz was a relative. Naomi told Ruth to go to Boaz and essentially ask him to be her husband. This act required courage, but Ruth had been created to be courageous. She had been bold from the beginning, as she showed when she journeyed to Bethlehem with Naomi. So this step would be nothing new for her.

That evening Ruth went and asked Boaz to marry her. He was surprised. Ruth was a younger woman who could have married anyone, but she was coming to him. He said yes.

Boaz and Ruth were married, and they had a son, whom they named Obed. Obed fathered Jesse, and Jesse fathered David—the same David who defeated Goliath and became king. This would be the same family tree that Jesus would be born into.

Naomi realized what most of us eventually learn, namely, that suffering is a part of our story, but it's not the end of our story. Ruth experienced that same truth. She was bold. She didn't shy away from who God made her to be. When she said to Naomi, "Your God will be my God" (Ruth 1:16 ICB), she was making a confession. She was leaving her old way of thinking and following God. She was determined to get to know him. She didn't shy away. And she was blessed because of it.

**Suffering is a part of our story, but it's not the end of our story.**

Our story is bigger than us. Our story affects generations and people groups. Don't shy away. Get to know Jesus intimately. Let the world see you. The course of history will be forever altered when you do.

chapter seven

# SUFFER WITH THE CITY

Professional football is an unusual sport. You spend months, even years, getting to know people: your teammates, coaches, and managers. And then, all of a sudden, they're gone. The turnover in the sport never sat well with me, and I didn't always know how to respond. I care deeply about people and relationships. But when you're competing with several guys for the same position, what do you do? Do you love them? Do you pray for them? Do you wish them the best? Or do you hope they get injured?

God had always opened doors for me. Whether it was through a teammate's injury, an opponent's mistake, or a coach's error, things always seemed to go my way. And this day was no different. I was three games into my third season with the Cardinals and had survived a coaching change, a general manager change, and a massive turnover of teammates. We were playing the New Orleans Saints in the famed Superdome, and I had just made my first sack of the season. I was excited. A few plays later, a teammate, a guy I was splitting time with on the field, went down with an injury. My feelings were simple. I acknowledged his pain, gave my condolences, and moved on. I had learned to quicken the mourning process. "Next man up" was the mentality you had to have to be successful, and so I put on that mask. At this particular moment feelings of sadness didn't even cross my mind.

"Sorry, bro," I said nonchalantly. "I'll be praying for you." But I didn't mean it.

He nodded his head, and I went back onto the field. *My* time had finally come. And this season, I thought, would be different. This was *my* opportunity, and I felt more than prepared. Little did I know things would take a turn for the worse.

God has an interesting way of humbling us, of reminding us who we are when we get too far off course. Sometimes it's sickness, other times it's demotion or injury. We were never created to carry the weight of the world on our own. We weren't made to worry either. See, that's the secret. We were made to seek Jesus. To put him on the throne of our hearts. To learn more about him in and through every situation. We were created to be one with our Creator. He wanted us so much that he came down to be with us. But even that wasn't enough. He wanted to take up residence in us, to make us his dwelling place, because we were created for a relationship with our Creator. And Scripture tells us he makes himself available:

> You will seek Me and find Me, when you search for Me with all your heart. (Jer. 29:13 NKJV)

> Draw near to God and He will draw near to you. (James 4:8 NKJV)

> I will remember their sins no more. (Heb. 8:12 ESV)

In Matthew 14, after feeding the five thousand, Jesus sent the disciples ahead of him on a boat so he could spend some time in prayer. When a storm came and he walked across the water toward them, they didn't even recognize him. But soon they would, and 1 Corinthians 13:12 tells us that one day we all will: "Now I know in part; then I shall know fully, even as I am fully known." God is beckoning us to him. He is waiting for us on our doorsteps. Fear not. You are already fully seen, fully known, and fully loved. Be you. You won't regret it.

After seeing my teammate carted off the field, I finished the first half and met up with him in the locker room at halftime. He was sitting on a table in the training room. Although he had suffered a season-ending injury, he seemed to be in good spirits. He knew God had good plans for him because he was a follower of Jesus. We talked briefly, and then I went to my locker to get some last-minute tips from the coaches. I returned to the field as focused as I'd ever been. I was prepared for everything. Except what happened a few moments later.

Minutes into the third quarter, after finally finding my groove, I took a wrong step and the rest was history. All of a sudden, on a routine play, I found myself at the bottom of a pile screaming in excruciating pain. I had broken my leg. My season was over. Less than an hour after my teammate's injury, and assuming this season would be different, Proverbs 16:9 was playing itself out in my life: "The heart of man plans his way, but the LORD establishes his steps" (ESV).

What do you do when you face disappointment? Do you cry? Do you mourn? Do you go into denial? So much was going through my mind at the time. I was unsure of how to feel. My adrenaline started to kick in and the pain temporarily subsided. I hobbled to the sideline, where the trainers began evaluating me. I didn't know how bad the injury was, plus the pain had gone away, so I wanted to go back in the game.

"Give me some Advil or something, guys. I need to get back out there," I told them.

But Advil wasn't going to do the trick this time. I was told I needed x-rays. My walking on a broken leg wasn't going to work, so they had to bring out a cart—the same one that had taken my teammate off the field not too long before. Now I could relate. Sadly, it would be the last time I would be on a football field that year.

It's one thing to see someone else in pain; it's a whole different thing to experience that pain yourself. You gain a whole lot of empathy. You gain perspective.

When I was fifteen years old, I went to Nigeria with my parents on a medical mission trip. There I interacted with another boy also named Sam. While he and I shared a name, our life experiences were extremely different. Sam barely had anything. His dingy, cream tank top hung over his bony, undernourished body. He looked as if he were eight years old, but he sounded very mature.

"How old are you?" I asked.

"Fifteen," he said.

I was shaken to my core. *He could be me,* I thought to myself. He really could have. I still had relatives in Nigeria: aunts and uncles, nieces and nephews. What made me different? Why did I get the better bargain in life? As we talked, I noticed something he had that I didn't. He had joy. Pure, undefiled joy. Joy in the midst of indescribable suffering.

I don't think Sam viewed himself as suffering. He walked with God. He didn't have a lot, but he had all he needed. As long as he had Jesus, he was okay.

I gave him my G-Shock watch that I had brought from the States. It dangled like a loose bracelet on his wrist, but he was appreciative. I was too. I learned something that day from Sam. I learned I can have joy even in the midst of my suffering.

Life experiences allow you to relate to people you never would have been able to relate with otherwise. Struggle does the same. As does doubt. As does pain. No one is perfect. Everyone has doubts. Our pain is a part of our story. But not only that, our pain allows us to be a part of other people's stories.

Jesus went through an immense amount of pain. He was beaten, bruised, spit at, stabbed, and whipped. He felt it all, so he can relate. He knows what it's like to struggle. He knows us deeply. And our pain allows us to get to know Jesus.

━

Who are you? What do you put your identity in? Is it your job? Your politics? Your kids? Your degree? It's not an easy question. But for the longest time, I always had an easy answer. I was a football player. I played in the NFL. It's a simple, straightforward answer. The subtlety behind it, though, was deadly. If you put your identity in what you do, what happens when that thing no longer identifies you? Yes, I was a football player. But after breaking my leg, I was no longer on the field. That ship had sailed, as the adage goes, and I had been left behind. So what was I now?

I've seen this phenomenon time and time again during my years in sports. One moment you're on top of the mountain, standing at the podium, answering questions about your heroics. The next, you disappear. Injuries will do that to you.

I was determined to be different. Deep down I knew I was more than an athlete. I was a human being, a child of God. I was experiencing something that every person will experience, if they haven't already; namely, suffering. Most guys disappear after a season-ending injury. They go home and do rehab, or if they stay in town, they are rarely seen. There can be a sense of disappointment, doubt, and confusion. But there can also be a different answer. They can choose to trust.

Somewhere between the day of my injury and when I had surgery, I realized something: my suffering was a part of my story. And not only that, it was a part of a bigger story; the human story. I was going to go through a good bit of suffering, but I didn't want to go through it alone. I wanted to share my suffering. I wanted to suffer with the city.

◆

In the Jewish tradition, when people lose a loved one, they sit *shibah*, a seven-day period in which people mourn their loss and accept condolences from others. After this, there is a less intense mourning period that, depending on the closeness of the one who was lost, can last between thirty days and a year.

In the days after my season-ending surgery, I had some good friends who sat shibah with me. They sat with me, ate with me, and encouraged me. They knew I had lost something I cared deeply about, and they didn't want me to go through it alone. They were living out Proverbs 17:17 in my life: "A friend loves at all times, and a brother is born for adversity" (NKJV). Sometimes we need friends who can mourn with us, who can remind us that our pain is a part of our story and that it's okay to cry, to mourn, to weep, and to be. My friends showed up for me.

One friend in particular really encouraged me during this process. After the brief mourning period, he gave me this advice: "Don't waste your suffering. Share it. Suffer with the city."

I knew exactly what he meant. All around the city of Phoenix people were hurting. People were in need of hope. Suffering is a human experience. No servant is greater than his master. We are followers of Jesus, and if he suffered, we will as well. It's to be expected. Pain, sorrow, joy, and frustration are all a part of our story. We all go through it.

Per my friend's advice, I found some people who were suffering in the city, and I sat with them. I mourned with them, and I allowed them to mourn with me. It was refreshing. From hospitals to homeless shelters, from schools to sandlots, any place where people needed help, I was there. I encouraged them in their journeys, and they encouraged me in mine.

This singular decision, the decision to be me, to mourn, to love, to not waste my pain, changed everything. I had so much fun that year. And I learned I was more than just a football player. I spent time encouraging the people around me and loving people who felt forgotten. My pain, my suffering, showed me who I really was. And I couldn't have been happier. For maybe the first time in my life, I was understanding the truth of James 1:2–4:

> Consider it pure joy, my brothers and sisters, whenever
> you face trials of many kinds, because you know that the

testing of your faith produces perseverance. Let perseverance finish its work so that you may be mature and complete, not lacking anything.

My pain, our pain, produces perseverance. Don't run from it, but embrace it. Your pain is a part of your story. It teaches you about who you are and allows you to get to know Jesus and his love for you.

Sometimes Jesus is our only hope. We spend a lot of our time amassing all kinds of things: fame, fortune, followers. But none of that really matters. The only thing that matters is Jesus.

A hymn proclaims, "On Christ, the solid Rock, I stand; all other ground is sinking sand." This song comes from one of Jesus' parables, stories that Jesus told to help his friends get to know him better. In this particular parable, he described two men who had very different reactions to their problems:

Everyone who hears these things I say and obeys them will be like a wise man. The wise man built his house on rock. It rained hard and the water rose. The winds blew and hit that house. But the house did not fall, because the house was built on rock. But the person who hears these things I teach and does not obey them is like a foolish man. The foolish man built his house on sand. It rained hard, the water rose, and the winds blew and hit that house. And the house fell with a big crash. (Matt. 7:24–27 ICB)

Storms are going to come in your life. They are a part of our story. But with Jesus, you can withstand the storm.

God is good. Period. We have our plans, our goals, our simplified thinking. Then there's God. A God who knitted us in our mothers' wombs, who knows the number of hairs on our heads. A God who, with a single phrase, can calm a storm: "Peace, be still" (Mark 4:39 NKJV). I feel as if God has been trying to tell us this ever since Adam and Eve were in the garden of Eden. "Peace, be still." In the midst of pain, in the midst of suffering, be still. Sit shibah. Mourn. "Be still, and know that I am God" (Ps. 46:10).

> Storms are going to come in your life. . . . But with Jesus, you can withstand the storm.

We spend so much time planning and worrying about a future we have no control over. Yet we have access to God, who is in complete control.

There is no need to fear. In your pain, in your suffering, have no fear. God is working it all out for your good and for his glory.

## chapter eight

# THUNDERBIRDS

I had just graduated from the University of Texas at Austin and been drafted 103rd overall by the Arizona Cardinals. I was ready to begin my career. The problem was, I had also just received a $25,000 postgraduate scholarship that had a two-year expiration date. Football was my thing, but learning was my love. I had graduated from the business honors program at one of the top universities in the country. I had been a double major and loved every minute of it. But now it appeared I was facing a choice between the NFL and free postgraduate work. I had a decision to make: play football, go to school, or find a way to do both. I chose the latter.

◆

While in college, when I heard about an award nicknamed the academic Heisman Trophy, I got excited. In college football, the Heisman Trophy is awarded to the best football player in the nation. Although I had lofty goals, that trophy was a little beyond my reach. So I aimed for one that seemed a little bit more attainable: the William V. Campbell Trophy.

I was a freshman, and this national award had just been won by a teammate. I asked him how he did it, and he made it seem pretty easy.

"Well," he said, "you're already at one of the top schools in the nation, so that's a plus. And you're in the business school. All you need to do is get into the honors program, and you'll give yourself a really good chance."

It sounded easy enough, but I knew the program had minimum grade point average requirements and that balancing both football and schoolwork would be tough.

"What if I get kicked out of the program?" I asked, thinking about the difficulty level.

"You won't," he replied with a smile. "Programs like that don't like kicking people out. It makes them look bad."

He was right on most accounts, but unfortunately there are always exceptions. And I would find that out the hard way.

＊

I was a semester into the business honors program (BHP). It was comprised of the best of the best. Many of the students received perfect scores on their SATs and were double and even triple majoring in premed and biomechanical engineering. Some were part of an even more selective program called Plan II, a fast-track path to success in the business world. In BHP, I was among the best and the brightest. But with this honor came high expectations. The minimum

GPA requirement was a 3.5 overall, meaning that Bs weren't going to cut it. But it was the fall, it was football season, and I was busy. I was taking a full course load while doing football full-time. Something had to give. And since I wasn't going to risk looking bad in front of my coaches, I didn't give the honors program my full attention.

*I've always been able to figure things out before,* I thought. *I'll be fine.*

I wasn't. At the end of the semester, I finished with an A, a B, and a C in my business courses. That's a 3.0, below the minimum for my major. That little difference created big problems.

I met with the dean of the business school, and he informed me of the unfortunate news. I was out of the program. I gave my usual football excuses, citing my busy in-season schedule, and assured him I would get my grades back up during the spring. He wasn't having it.

"I'm sorry, Sam," he began. "But even if you have more time in the spring, what happens next year during football season and the year after that? Everyone is busy. Many of our students work multiple jobs, have internship obligations and family issues that are pulling at them as well. I can make no exception for you. I'm sorry."

And with that, my major and my dreams of winning the William V. Campbell Trophy were gone.

～

Have you ever had your dreams crushed, seemingly stolen from you because of a seemingly unfair situation? How did you feel? How did you respond? I felt pretty miserable. I had missed out on a great opportunity.

I told my teammate what happened. I told him I was pretty disappointed in myself and the situation and wanted a second chance. Another opportunity to show who I really was. Some of my teammates hadn't been taking school seriously, so I hadn't either. But that really wasn't me. I knew if given another chance, I would be able to not only win this award but also do what I love: learn from the best teachers in the world.

Before I finished talking, my teammate shouted excitedly, "Appeal it! Appeal the decision. I heard about this process where, based on extenuating circumstances, you can appeal a decision and have them revisit it."

It sounded like a great idea, so I wrote a letter, explaining what had happened and why my grades were poor. I talked about football and my intense schedule. But my appeal was denied, and I was devastated. *Well*, I reasoned, *at least I'm still in the business school.*

I told my dad the news, trying to hide my disappointment, but my dad knows me really well. After I finished, he offered up another idea. "Appeal it again," he said calmly.

"*What?* Dad, they just rejected my first appeal. Why on earth would they accept a second appeal, let alone even consider it?"

He reminded me of who I was. The people closest to you will do that. He reminded me that I was more than a football player, and the business school needed to see that. He reminded me of times in the past when things looked bleak, but God made a way. He reminded me of how I got into the program in the first place. He reminded me to be me, not what everyone else expected of me. And he reminded me of who God is.

"It can't hurt, son. Appeal it again, but this time, be you."

So I did. And I was.

I wrote out my second appeal, but this time I took a different approach. I wasn't trying to please or impress anyone. I was honest. I told them about the mistakes I'd made and how I hadn't taken my work seriously. I told them how I had fallen into the trap of complacency. I told them who I was, how I was a man of my word. I met with the dean again and gave him my word that they would not regret it if they allowed me back into the program.

I took a major risk. I risked looking silly. I risked looking desperate. I risked looking like a little kid. But I was me.

And before I submitted the appeal, I prayed. I prayed that God would open a door for me to get back into the program. And that is exactly what he did. But he used my hands to open the door.

Winter break was over, and it was time for classes to begin. I hadn't heard back on my second appeal, and the only information I had was a rejection letter with instructions to drop out of my honors courses and sign up for regular courses. But I hadn't dropped out, and the deadline to enroll in any new classes had passed. I felt pretty bleak because something I had put my identity in—academic prowess—seemed to have been taken away.

As I walked into the building, I prayed. I was frustrated. I was sad. But I was praying. As I was having my miniconversation with God, the Holy Spirit nudged me and told me to wait a little and hold the door open for the woman behind me. Usually, when I get in one of these moods, I don't bother with such niceties. But this time I listened.

I walked to the door, opened it, and waited for her to walk up the steps, down the patio, and through the door.

"Wow, thank you so much," she said. "You didn't have to do that."

"No problem," I replied.

I started to walk down the hall toward the academic offices, and I noticed the woman was walking in the same direction. We both strode down the hall and around the corner toward the BHP program office.

*Interesting*, I thought. *Maybe she's a graduate student.* I didn't think too much about it until I walked inside the office, where she had walked in a few moments before me. There was a small waiting room in front, but she wasn't there. I wondered where she went as I approached the receptionist and told her about my issue.

"I'm not sure what classes I'm supposed to go to," I said. "I appealed my BHP decision and sent an email to a lady named Ruby, but I haven't heard back."

"No problem," the receptionist said. "She just walked in. I'll let her know you're here."

A few moments later, a woman came out. The same woman I had held the door for a few minutes earlier, the same woman who had emailed me about my first appeal being rejected, the same woman who I sent the second appeal to, and the same woman I was praying would show me favor.

I was startled. I think she was too, judging by the look on her face.

"Oh," she exclaimed. "Uh, nice to meet you, Sam. We're still doing our final review of your second appeal, but we should have an answer for you by the end of the day."

"What should I do in the meantime?" I asked. "The only classes I'm signed up for are the ones I've been kicked out of."

"Well," she began, "just go to the ones you are registered for."

So I did. A few hours later, I checked my email and saw a message from Ruby: "Congratulations, your second appeal has been accepted. Please meet with your adviser to discuss the requirements."

And Ruby was to be my adviser. From that point on, we formed a bond. My friends and I treated her like family. We loved her, cared for her, told her about Jesus, and made sure she knew she was loved.

I went on to graduate from the business honors program and form lifelong bonds with the faculty and classmates I met on that first day, the day I didn't know where to go. I also won the Campbell Trophy plus the $25,000 postgraduate scholarship that came with it. I was the second winner of that award in the school's history.

God opened the door. He just happened to have used my hands to do it. I was me. Even in the disappointment, I was me. And I had people around me who reminded me of who I was. We all need friends like that. People who remind us of who we are and who God is. God is still in the business of doing miracles. He is the same yesterday, today, and forever. He has never changed and never will. The God who brought Joseph out of bondage and into the king's court is the same God who can free you from your situation, no matter what you're going through. Your only requirement, God's only ask, is that you get to know him intimately. Get to know your Creator. In doing so, you will get to know yourself.

That trophy stands in two places. In the hall of honor at the University of Texas and at my parents' house. Every time I go home, I'm reminded not of the trophy but of the people who believed in me. The people who showed me who I am.

※

As I was entering my second season in the NFL, I had yet to use the $25,000 postgraduate scholarship that came with winning the Campbell Trophy. I'm not a math major, but free is free, and I wanted to take advantage of the opportunity. My job was physically taxing, but it had a four-month off-season. Still, time was working against me as I was nearing its two-year expiration date. I didn't want to let this gift go to waste, so I started searching for postgraduate programs that would allow me to take classes part time.

My first choice was Stanford. That was an easy choice. I called the admissions office and told them who I was and that I was looking to enroll in a part-time MBA program during the off-season. I figured they would be happy to accommodate an NFL player.

They weren't.

"I'm sorry," the admissions person replied, "but we only do full-time MBAs. To make this work, you're going to have to quit your job for a few years while you complete the program."

Well, that clearly wasn't going to happen. I was playing in the NFL, which was a once-in-a-lifetime opportunity. So I really had only two choices: forgo the scholarship or keep looking. I chose the latter.

I was pretty dejected after my call to Stanford, but I have a one-track mind. When I focus on something, I put all my effort into it. I don't usually have a backup plan, especially if that backup plan consists of a school I never heard of in a place not known for its academics. Boy, was I in for a surprise.

The Thunderbird School of Global Management is a mouthful, but it is also the school with the #1 ranked international MBA in the world. And it happened to be in Glendale, Arizona, a thirty-four-minute drive from my home in Phoenix. I know the exact time because I made that drive every Monday through Thursday, from January to May, for four years. I had the timing down to a science because our off-season workouts ended forty minutes before class started. That meant I had six minutes to shower, change, and get to the car. Needless to say, I was smelly for a few classes.

I'll never forget the drive to school. But what was even more memorable was how I got to Thunderbird in the first place.

I had just been drafted by the Cardinals and was putting some roots down in Phoenix. One day I was at a sushi bar with a friend. I'm not a big sushi fan, but this restaurant was different. Its Asian fusion cuisine and awesome chef made my night. We ordered our food and I prayed before the meal. Our dinner was over, and I was sitting alone at the bar while my friend went to the restroom, when all of a sudden a short white guy turned to me and asked, "Sorry to bother you, but how did you find God?"

I wondered who this guy was and how he knew I was a Christian. I checked the television in the bar to see if maybe it was showing an interview I had done with the Cardinals or something, but there was a baseball game in progress.

I didn't know how to answer the question, so I responded the best way I knew how: "Well, I didn't find God. God found me."

Let me pause here and say that I think many people look at Christians and wonder how they came to faith. How they got saved. The answer is that it is all by the grace of God. If anyone tells you different, they're lying. Ephesians 2:4–9 tells me that God knows me. He knows who I am and what I've done. He has forgiven my sins and given me new life. And he wants to extend that new life to anyone who wants it. Anyone who believes. Romans 10:9 assures us, "If you declare with your mouth, 'Jesus is Lord,' and believe in your heart that God raised him from the dead, you will be saved." That freedom is available for anyone. Even the guy sitting next to you at a sushi bar.

"I knew it!" he exclaimed. "You're like the fifth person I've met who said that."

He said his name was Max, and he was a native of Phoenix. He went on to tell me how he had seen me pray over the meal and couldn't help but wonder. He was in a unique place in life and felt God was tugging on his heart, but he didn't really know how to feel about it. He explained that Jesus had never been a big part of his life. He never really went to church except for Christmas and occasionally Easter and didn't have many Christian friends.

I love Jesus and I love people, so I offered a proposition. I told him I was pretty sure I had a Bible in the car that I planned to give to one of my teammates. But if he was willing to wait, I would go get it.

Max said he'd wait.

But as I was walking out of the restaurant, I remembered I had left the Bible at the practice facility in Tempe. I apologized and started to walk away. But before I could leave, Max asked if I would check anyway. I was sure there was no point in doing it, but I halfheartedly agreed. I opened the trunk of my car and began searching under some clothes when I felt a rectangular box. *This can't be*, I thought. But it was. The Bible I was sure I had put in my locker was somehow in my car. I was so excited.

I had received some Bibles at a Fellowship of Christian Athletes event earlier in the week, and they were brand new. I ran back into the restaurant and gave Max the good news. He was thrilled, even more so when he saw the cover: *The Competitor's Bible.*

Max said, "I feel like I've been a competitor my whole life. This is perfect! But where do I start?"

I knew the perfect place. Max and I became friends that day. And we made an agreement to meet weekly. I would teach him about the Bible, and he would teach me about the city.

It was during one of our weekly get-togethers that he told

me about the Thunderbird School of Global Management. He mentioned it was a top-tier school and that people came from all over the world because of its reputation.

This sounded too good to be true, so I asked one of my friends from college if she knew anything about the school, and she confirmed everything Max had said. So I did some more digging and realized they were right. Then I took the thirty-four-minute drive to visit the campus and to find out more. As soon as I walked onto the grounds I fell in love. There were students from all around the world. Every language I could imagine was being spoken. It was a dream come true.

I love people. I love different cultures. And I love learning. This was the perfect mix. I applied and was accepted, and my journey began.

I graduated from Thunderbird a few years later and formed several lifelong relationships that span the globe. I told my teammates about my MBA, and they applauded me for it. I was seen. I was known. I was loved. Now, it's your turn.

━●━

Being you isn't convenient. It takes stepping out on a limb, taking a risk, and being okay with the results. Though fear tried to hold me back, faith eventually took hold. I formed an entirely new set of relationships and got to tell more than a few friends about what God was doing in my life and about who Jesus was.

In Matthew 28, Jesus gave his final commandment to his followers. "Go," he said, "and make disciples of all nations"

(v. 19). I had a school in my backyard that housed people from nearly every nation, so I went. And I made disciples. I led Bible studies, developed friendships, and loved on people who had never heard about Jesus. And I couldn't have been happier.

**Though fear tried to hold me back, faith eventually took hold.**

In Ephesians 2:10, Paul wrote, "For we are his workmanship, created in Christ Jesus for good works, which God prepared beforehand, that we should walk in them" (ESV). When I arrived in Arizona, I soon learned how God had prepared the way for me. And by being me, I was walking right in his will. He received the glory, the people around me benefitted, and the world around me thrived. I now know that I am more than a football player, but I guess I always was. I'm a child of God, an evangelist, a student, a son, a friend, and so much more. You are too. Never forget it.

What gifts has God given you that you are neglecting? What spaces in your life are you ignoring because of fear? Face them, and watch God do the rest.

## chapter nine

# ALLERGIC TO EXERCISE

People always wonder how we hear from God. He speaks in many ways, but you have to listen. He speaks through events, through other people, through dreams, through his Word, and sometimes through a still, small voice, like he did for Elijah.

> And behold, the LORD passed by, and a great and strong wind tore the mountains and broke in pieces the rocks before the LORD, but the LORD was not in the wind. And after the wind an earthquake, but the LORD was not in the earthquake. And after the earthquake a fire, but the LORD was not in the fire. And after the fire the sound of a low whisper. (1 Kings 19:11–12 ESV)

In 1 Kings 19, the prophet Elijah was being pursued by an evil king. Elijah had just mocked the evil king and his army and showed them that God is the one and only

God. He was on cloud nine. But then something happened. After slaughtering all the evil prophets who were there, you would think Elijah would have been rejoicing. He wasn't. As a matter of fact, he went into hiding. Why? Because the evil king's wicked wife had heard what Elijah had done and wanted him to pay for it. She promised to avenge the death of her prophets within twenty-four hours.

What would you do if you were in this situation? You just performed an amazing miracle in front of thousands. You showed the world that God is real, and God showed up for you in a miraculous way. You defeated your enemy in impressive fashion. You would be ready to take on the world, right? Not Elijah. Once he heard the queen's plan to kill him, he ran.

Everybody has weaknesses. Mine showed up in the middle of a high-intensity situation. It was the first game of my second year in the NFL. It was also my first season as a full-time starter. I had worked harder than ever before to prepare for this moment. I was ready. I was in shape. I was focused. Every detail mattered. And in this case, every detail was essential to the team's success. The stakes were high. The game was on the line. We were going into the fourth quarter against a strong opponent. I had just made a huge stop in the game and ran to the sideline to celebrate with my teammates when all of a sudden one of them stopped me.

"Bro," he said. "What's going on with your face?"

Sidelines and locker rooms can be interesting places. I

figured he was making a joke to alleviate the pressure of the situation. People do that sometimes. So I dismissed the comment, getting my focus back on the game. But then he tapped me again.

"Bro, I'm serious," he said. "Your face is . . . swollen."

As he was speaking, he gestured to one of the team doctors to take a look. I was confused. My eyebrows were itching a little, so I figured some grass had gotten caught in my helmet. But then it got worse. Nearly every part of my body started to itch and break out in hives.

As word spread, all eyes were on me. Not because of my amazing achievement on the field, but because everyone was trying to see what was happening to me on the sideline. Once again, like all those years ago at the Wednesday evening youth service, I felt ashamed, embarrassed, and wished I could run into the closest restroom stall. But I couldn't.

The itching continued.

The hives spread to my arms, chest, and even my lips. It felt like everyone was keyed in, not on the game but on me. I hated it. I was being seen at my most vulnerable state. I tried to put my helmet on and run back on the field, but the doctor wouldn't allow it. My face was swollen, my eyes were swollen, even my lips were swollen.

I received a shot from an EpiPen, and the swelling began to subside. I was eager to get back on the field. I finally pulled away from the doctor, but only after he had asked about the itchiness in my face, lips, and throat. The last question caught my attention.

"Why does it matter if my throat is itching?" I asked.

"If your throat is itching," he explained, "that means the swelling has reached your esophagus. And that means that you won't be able to breathe."

Now I was scared. But my shame at the time overrode my fear. I threw on my helmet, ran onto the field, and didn't take it off again until I reached the locker room after the game was over.

The swelling subsided, but the same episode happened at the same time in every game for the rest of the season. After a series of tests and studies, the doctors, dermatologists, and internists concluded I was suffering from a condition called exercise-induced angioedema. That's a fancy way of saying I'm allergic to exercise. It's almost laughable to hear that a professional athlete, someone who exercises for a living, could be allergic to exercise. But I am. I was exerting my full energy on every play in every game, and it reached a point where my body could no longer cooperate. The body keeps its own score.

Once again I resorted to hiding. That year I started wearing long-sleeved shirts under my pads and a dark face shield on my face mask so people would have a hard time seeing me. After games, if the swelling was bad, I waited until everyone finished showering before I took one. The symptoms always seemed to get worse when people saw me. So I ran. I hid.

━━━

Moses did something similar after he discovered his true identity. He was a Hebrew raised in an Egyptian household.

But not just any Egyptian home, he was raised in the palace of the king.

At the time of Moses' birth, the new king was not a fan of the Hebrews. Because they had come to Egypt in great numbers, he feared they would revolt and overtake the Egyptians. So he oppressed them. He made them slaves and treated them with contempt. He feared them so much he decreed all newborn Hebrew boys be killed. And along came Moses.

Upon his birth, Moses' mother hid him for three months and then put him in a basket and placed it among the reeds along the bank of the Nile, hoping to save his life. The king's daughter often bathed in the river, and that day she stumbled upon the boy. When she saw him, she fell in love with him and adopted him. Thus Moses became a part of the royal family. But even though he lived in a royal household, Moses knew his identity.

One day, when he saw a slave driver beating a Hebrew slave, he got angry. So angry, the Bible says, that he killed the slave driver and hid the body in the sand. The next day, when Moses saw two Hebrews fighting each other, he asked why they were fighting. One of the men responded, "Who made you ruler and judge over us? Are you thinking of killing me as you killed the Egyptian?" (Ex. 2:14).

Moses didn't think anyone had seen what he had done, but he was wrong. He knew the king would soon find out and have him killed. Moses was afraid, so he ran.

Being seen can be hard. It can come with countless emotions, fears, and doubts. There can be a lot to cope with. But God does not make mistakes. After Moses fled, he was sitting at a well when his true self came out again. Nobody can hide who they really are forever.

Moses had fled to Midian and didn't know anyone there. One day, when seven daughters of a Midianite priest came to get some water for their father's sheep and a few shepherds tried to harass them, Moses came to their rescue. The girls' father heard what he did and invited Moses to stay with him for as long as he wanted.

**Nobody can hide who they really are forever.**

Fast-forward forty years, God brought Moses to a burning bush and told him it was time for him to walk in his identity. It was time for him to free the Hebrew slaves. So he did.

❧

I continued to play that season and for several seasons after, but only after I developed a new practice before each snap while I was on the field: I would pray, *Jesus, I need you.* I had no choice. I understood the severity of my condition. I knew that if the swelling got bad enough, my throat could swell up, and I would suffocate.

As I prayed and listened for God's voice during those games, I would hear God say, *Fear not, I am with you.* It's funny, amid all the noise and the thousands of screaming fans, even with my opponents standing directly in front of my face, all I could hear was God's voice. That gave me comfort. And I learned to seek his comfort regularly, not only in between snaps. Even now I talk to God often. I'm learning the discipline of listening to that still, small voice.

To that whisper that reminds me not to be afraid, because he is with me, he is for me, and he is proud of me.

Often the prospect of being seen for who we really are can be frightening. But what we learn *during* our times of hiding is what matters most. Because God knows us and loves us, we have an opportunity to *be us* in those times when we most want to hide. To be who God created us to be.

Learn to pray. Learn to be still and hear God's whisper in the midst of all the chaos around you. Learn to listen.

How do you do this? Study Scripture. Read the words of Jesus when he walked the earth. Meditate on the Word of God. Listen to the Holy Spirit. Follow the Prince of Peace. "My sheep listen to my voice; I know them, and they follow me" (John 10:27). Hear the voice of God. He will never leave you. He sees you, even when you don't see yourself.

## chapter ten

# PRISON WITH
# THE PRESIDENT

I believe God puts us in places for reasons and seasons. I finished my time in Arizona and was a free agent. During my transition, I prayed for three things: an opportunity to make an impact on the football field, a chance to make a change in my community, and good weather. Every day I prayed for these things, motivated by James 4:2: "You do not have because you do not ask God."

Free agency is an interesting experience. Every year some players sign massive contracts and become multi-millionaires. My story was different.

For the first three weeks of free agency, no one called me. My agent had shared a list of teams that were interested in signing me, but none were making any moves. Early on he mentioned Chicago as a possibility, but I dismissed it because they ran a different type of defense than what I was used to. Plus, it was cold in Chicago, and I was praying for good weather. I was sure it wasn't where God was going to take me. I was wrong.

I don't know if you've ever been in a position where you're waiting for a call. Whether it's for a job or for a school you applied to or for a friend or family member who's received some bad news, waiting can be stressful. At least it was for me. Several times I thought maybe my phone was messed up, but it was working just fine.

While I was in class, I was reading about several teams that were looking for people who played my position. I researched their salary caps and who was on their rosters. I trusted that my agent was doing his job, but I couldn't help but be curious.

Finally, one day, I received a call. I didn't recognize the number, but I answered it anyway. John Fox, the head coach of the Chicago Bears, was on the other end. I was surprised, confused, and relieved all at the same time. I had admired Coach Fox for years. He told me the Bears were interested in me and that I would have an opportunity to compete for a starting spot. That was all I wanted.

I was excited that God had answered my prayer. (Although not about the weather!) Though I loved my time in Phoenix, I wanted something more. And Chicago was indeed more. More scrutiny, more opportunity, more problems. In marketing classes in college, we talked about finding a need and filling it. Chicago had a need. And God was going to use me to help fill it.

Chicago is known for its violence. In the early 2000s it was given the nickname Chi-raq because more people died each year in the city than in the Iraq War. But I was excited to go there because I knew there was a need I might help fill. People needed hope. People needed smiles. The way I saw it, the people there needed me. The real me. And by the grace of God, I was finally starting to be me. God had always given me a desire to go to places no one else wanted to go and to love the people no one else wanted to love. I wanted to make an impact. So when Coach Fox called and offered me a job in this city, I said yes.

My time in Chicago was interesting to say the least. I was promised a chance to compete for a starting spot, but it seemed there was nothing I could do to earn it. Though I wanted to make an impact in the community, there was a part of me that put that desire on a back burner. All I cared about then was my image. I wanted to prove to the Cardinals general manager that he had made a mistake when he didn't renew my contract. I wanted to show the world, on a national stage, that I was enough. I wanted to show my new coaches, new teammates, and new city that they were getting one of the best football players in the country.

But I was more than just a football player. And God needed to show me that.

Year one came and went. And though I didn't start every game, I made the team and made an impact on the field. It was now time to expand my focus to the community around me. And I knew just the way to do it: throw a party.

I love parties. I love getting people together and having

a good time. Whether it's at my house, at a restaurant, or in a classroom, I love seeing people come together and get to know one another. I'm what people call a convener. There's something special about seeing people come out of their shells.

Jesus loved parties too. After all, his first miracle was at a wedding reception. The host ran out of the good stuff, so Jesus turned water into wine. Not just any wine but the best wine. It was so good that even the party planner noticed: "The master of the wedding called the bridegroom and said to him, 'People always serve the best wine first. Later, after the guests have been drinking a lot, they serve the cheaper wine. But you have saved the best wine till now'" (John 2:9–10 ICB).

Jesus loved welcoming people and loving them wholeheartedly. It's easy to be you when you know you're loved and accepted, so I always tried to create environments like that.

My first attempt at this in Chicago was during the Sam Acho Celebrity Waiter Night. The goals of the event were simple. First, it was to raise money for Living Hope Ministries, a nonprofit my parents started to help hurting people in Nigeria. Second, I wanted to give Bears supporters an opportunity to see the players for who they really are: human beings who love what they do, love having fun, and love each other. So I invited every guy on the team; not one player was left out. And if that wasn't enough, I invited many of the coaches too. Everyone's job was to be stand-in servers for the night and compete with each other for tips and show off their personalities.

The stage was set, and I thought I had all my bases covered. That is, until I ran into someone at a mall two weeks before the event who I thought didn't even know who I was: George McCaskey, the chairman of the Chicago Bears and the son of team owner Virginia McCaskey. Mrs. McCaskey's father, George Halas, was one of the founders of the NFL and the founder of the Chicago Bears more than a hundred years ago.

As the chairman of the team, George oversaw all things Chicago Bears. From on the field to in the community, it was all important to him. So when I encountered him that day, I was met with a stern face and a serious question.

"I hear you're hosting an event," he began. "Why didn't I get an invite?"

I didn't know if he was being serious or if he was joking. Anyone who knows George knows he has a sense of humor, but at the time I didn't know him very well. What I did know, however, was how to be a good host. So I invited him. I told him the date, time, and location, and let him know that it would be an honor to have him there.

Not only did George show up, but he was the first one there. On top of that, he wore my jersey. I was floored. Since he came early, we had a chance to get to know each other. We talked together, fellowshipped together, and served food together. I learned a lot about George that day. I learned about his friends, his family, his likes and dislikes. And a bond was formed. Not entirely because of our conversations, but because he showed up. No shame, no pride, no ego. He just showed up. He was invited to the party and he came.

What invitations have you received that are awaiting your

acceptance? What opportunities have you been given that you're contemplating whether to go or not? Show up. Don't be ashamed or proud. Just show up. Who knows what miracles may happen? Someone might just turn water into wine.

**What invitations have you received that are awaiting your acceptance? . . . Don't be ashamed or proud. Just show up.**

That time with George changed everything. Because of his willingness to show up, trust was built between us. And this trust would be needed just one year later when turmoil struck our team.

✦

We were two weeks into the 2017 season, and everyone was up in arms about the national anthem. A year earlier, quarterback Colin Kaepernick of the San Francisco 49ers had begun to take a knee during the singing of the national anthem as a peaceful protest against some injustices he was seeing in America.

"I am not going to stand up to show pride in a flag for a country that oppresses black people and people of color," he said. "To me, this is bigger than football and it would be selfish on my part to look the other way. There are bodies in the street and people [responsible are] getting paid leave and getting away with murder."[2]

Colin was making a statement, and people were listening. So much so that his protests, along with those of many other professional athletes, received a direct response from the president of the United States. That's when things got really interesting.

Colin's statement and his subsequent actions were bold. He knew he would be asked about them before every game and during every interview. He knew he would have to have an answer. He knew he was going to be ripped apart by the media and torn to pieces by the fans. He didn't care. This was his opportunity to address the injustices he was seeing.

And soon I was about to get mine.

On a Friday night, just after practice, I was watching the news when I saw it: "Wouldn't you love to see one of these NFL owners, when somebody disrespects our flag, to say, 'Get that [SOB] off the field right now. Out! He's fired! He's fired!'" said President Donald Trump.[3]

At first I laughed, shrugging it off as yet another callous comment from the president. But then I began to feel really angry. *He's talking about my teammates, my brothers. He could be talking about* me.

I don't know about you, but justice is big for me. Speaking up for those who can't speak up for themselves has been one of my mottos for a long time. And I felt that what President Trump had done, what he had said, was an attack on the people closest to me.

But if you think I was angry, you should have seen my teammates' faces during our meeting the next morning. They were livid! Many of them were up in arms. How could the president of the United States say something so disrespectful? We debated among ourselves about what to do because something had to be done. Later that night something would.

After hearing the president's statement, many NFL players felt like taking a knee during the national anthem. We felt we had to do something to show the president and the world that we were united. Not just as a team but as a unit, as a collective body. We wanted to show that we had each other's backs. We were less than twenty-four hours from kickoff and emotions were sky-high. What were we going to do? I didn't have an answer then, but I knew I would have to find one soon.

On the night before the game, things were going as planned. I arrived at the team hotel, checked into my room, visited the chapel, then started to walk to our team meeting when I was cornered by three people: the head coach, the general manager, and the chairman of the Chicago Bears. They stopped me dead in my tracks. I thought about trying to get away because I don't like being caught off guard and not being prepared for a situation, but there was no running away from this one. John Fox, Ryan Pace, and George McCaskey surrounded me. Their question was simple: What are you guys going to do tomorrow during the national anthem?

I don't know if you've ever been caught off guard like this and been met with a question you had no good answer to. Well, that was me in this moment. I wasn't a team captain. I was just me, a guy who talked to everyone on the team, knew everyone on the team, and had the pulse of everyone on the team. These three men knew this, and so they decided to ask me about the plan for game day.

I said to them, "I don't know what we're going to do tomorrow. We're still trying to decide on that. But what I do know is that, whatever we do, we need to know you guys have our backs. That we have your full support."

George McCaskey rarely attended team meetings. So if the guys were to see him there, they would know something was up. Coach Fox and Ryan Pace had voiced their support for us earlier in the day, but guys wanted to know that support was coming from the top too.

I said to George, "If you're going to speak to the team tonight, we need to know one thing. Do you have our backs?"

I didn't get an immediate answer. I think George was surprised by how frank I was and needed time to figure out what, if anything, he was going to say to the team.

A few minutes later, when the meeting began, Coach Fox reiterated his support for us, as did Ryan Pace. Then everyone turned to see what George was going to do.

I have never been a chairman of anything, and certainly not the chairman of a professional sports team, but I can imagine George was being pulled in all directions. He had fans writing letters and expressing their feelings about the organization. He had staff to keep in mind. He had family and the family tradition he definitely felt pressured to uphold. He had coaches with their viewpoints. And he had players he valued highly and who are the faces of the franchise. Yes, George was being pulled in all kinds of directions.

He walked up in front of the team and cleared his throat. He told us that although his personal desire was that we stand for the anthem, he would support us no matter what we did. His only request was that whatever we do, we do it together. With that, the meeting adjourned.

Usually, after our night meetings ended, we would grab a snack, joke a bit, then go to bed. But there would be no snacking this night. No joking either. All we did was meet with each other. We met in walkways and hallways, elevators and empty rooms. I needed to figure out a plan moving forward, and to do that I needed everyone's input because without input, there can be very little buy-in. So I got to work.

After hours of discussions with nearly everyone on the team, we still had no consensus. I was stressed out that night, unsure of what the next day would look like. Then I was reminded of 1 Peter 5:7, "Cast all your anxiety on him because he cares for you." That verse resonated with me. God reminded me that I had no need to worry because he had it under control. He knew exactly where I was, exactly how I felt, and exactly what was going on. I was so worried because I felt as if all the weight of the decision was on my shoulders—a decision I didn't ask to be a part of making, a decision that could negatively affect others' perception of me and my team for years to come. And I needed to be reminded that everything was going to be okay. After reading that verse, I finally got some rest, trusting that God would provide an answer. And he did.

> God reminded me that I had no need to worry because he had it under control.

There are certain passages in the Bible that I rely on when I start to feel anxious and need answers. Philippians 4:6–7 is one of them: "Do not be anxious about anything, but in every situation, by prayer and petition, with thanksgiving, present your requests to God. And the peace of God, which transcends all understanding, will guard your hearts and your minds in Christ Jesus."

If you read Paul's words carefully, you'll notice something I used to always miss. Though I go to this verse when I need answers, the promise the apostle gave isn't something physical, but peace. The promise is peace. I think Jesus promises us peace because he knows that the peace of his presence is better than anything we could receive. I experienced this peace firsthand when I went to sleep that night and when I woke up the next morning. I was no longer worried about what the day held. I was postured in peace.

I walked into the locker room two hours before the game and entered into the moment of truth. The first person to approach me was Josh Sitton, a Pro Bowl offensive guard who had just signed with the team from Green Bay.

"What's the plan, Sam?" he asked.

Josh was rough. He was a white guy from Pensacola, Florida, who grew up country. He was six feet three and weighed 335 pounds. He didn't really empathize with Colin and felt the national anthem wasn't the proper time to protest. If he had his way, we would all stand with our hands over our hearts as usual.

Then Benny Cunningham walked in. He was a five-foot-ten special teams ace from Tennessee. Benny was black and empathized with Colin and the people Colin was advocating for. Benny was playing for the St. Louis Rams in 2014 when Michael Brown, an African American teenager, was shot and killed by a white police officer in Ferguson, Missouri. Months later, when the officer was not indicted, many Rams players protested by entering the stadium with their hands up in the air and wearing "Hands Up, Don't Shoot" T-shirts that many protesters had been wearing days prior. At the time Benny had decided not to protest, but he had regretted his decision ever since. He finally had an opportunity to right this perceived wrong, and he didn't want to miss it.

"What are we doing, Acho?" he asked sternly.

It was decision time. But I felt an immense amount of peace.

"We are locking arms," I replied. "We're gonna show everyone that we're together and that nothing anyone says or does can divide us."

The word spread throughout the team. We went on the field, locked arms during the anthem, and played together as a team. We won the game, but it's what happened afterward that changed everything.

After the victory celebration ended, I was sitting at my locker when I saw George McCaskey make a beeline toward me. Before I had a chance to react, he was standing directly in front of me. He shook my hand, congratulated me on the win, and applauded how we handled the anthem. Then he made me an offer.

"Sam, I don't want this to be the last time we talk about these issues. If this is something you guys really care about, come up to my office, and let's see how we can figure out a solution. My door is always open."

Most owners would never have offered. But George was different. He cared about people. He cared about justice. George had learned to be himself. He refused to conform to the mindset of his peers. He was a loving, caring, thoughtful individual. That's why he had shown up to my event the previous year. And because he showed up, I showed up. Life is usually reciprocated that way.

The first time I went to George's office, I came with a few ideas I had gotten from a friend who believed that experience is one of the best ways to learn. So I walked in with three proposals: police, prison, and hip-hop.

One proposal for each of the three months left in the season. I made my offer and waited for his response. He said yes to all three. So we set dates and began our adventure.

❦

If we wanted to help the people of Chicago, we needed a better understanding of the city. We needed to get our hands dirty. You rarely learn anything from far away, so we figured the best way to try to make changes was to learn.

For the police part of my proposal, George had connections in the police department from having worked with them for years. I knew where to begin for the prison part, because I had visited a couple of prisons the year before and had connections to some local facilities.

We wanted to get a better understanding of what police officers went through, what prisoners went through, and allow ourselves to look at the world through a different lens. So we did a police ride-along in Englewood, one of the most dangerous neighborhoods in Chicago. After that we visited the Kewanee Life Skills Re-Entry Center in Kewanee, Illinois. It's a facility for people who have been in prison and are now on their way back to society.

For the hip-hop part, well, the recording artist Lecrae was an easy choice. His music addressed many of the social justice issues we were trying to tackle. Plus I was going to one of his concerts and decided to invite George.

I learned a lot from my time with George. We laughed together, cried together, learned together. He was himself, and I was in awe of that. His being himself allowed me to be me. After those three events, I figured he would've had enough. He hadn't.

"What's next?" he asked excitedly.

"I don't know yet," I said, "but I can assure you it's gonna be an adventure."

And it was.

Our next trip was to visit the National Museum of African American History and Culture in Washington, DC. We learned so much at that place. We got a chance to look at American history through an African American lens. It was special. While in DC, we visited Howard University, a historically black university, to look at some of America's social justice issues from a different perspective. We also met with Eugene Scott, an African American CNN political reporter who had been hired just a week before Donald Trump announced his presidential campaign.

From there we went to Minneapolis, where the Super Bowl was to be played, and met with Justice Alan Page, a Hall of Fame NFL defensive lineman who was also the first African American state supreme court justice of Minnesota. Justice Page had an exhibit of historic artifacts from US history: a slave-made brick from the original construction of the White House to signs that promulgated segregation in the 1950s. We talked with him and gained a better understanding of some of America's often untold history.

Then George invited me to the owners' Super Bowl party. I was his plus-one. It was fun, but I think I throw better parties. I reciprocated by inviting him to the Louisiana State Penitentiary, the largest maximum-security prison in the United States.

I visited the Louisiana State Penitentiary earlier in March 2016. Before that I had never set foot in a prison. But one Sunday I heard a sermon on Matthew 25 and couldn't forget it. In that passage, Jesus said:

> For I was hungry and you gave me something to eat, I was thirsty and you gave me something to drink, I was a stranger and you invited me in, I needed clothes and you clothed me, I was sick and you looked after me, *I was in prison and you came to visit me.* . . . . Truly I tell you, whatever you did for one of the least of these brothers and sisters of mine, you did for me." (vv. 35–36, 40, emphasis mine)

Jesus loves "the least of these," those forgotten and cast out by society. I knew that truth about the poor, but I had yet to realize that truth about the prisoner.

My church had a Christmastime prison ministry for which we sent gifts to people in prison, but I wanted to do more than just spend a few hours wrapping gifts for people I would never see. I wanted to spend time with followers of Christ who were behind bars. Soon after this thought popped in my mind, I was invited to visit the penitentiary by both the pastor who gave the sermon and the chaplain for the team. I said yes.

People in prison get a bad rap. The United States uses the penal system as a way to lock up people and throw away the key. Sometimes justice is served, but sometimes it's not. The world is full of broken people. And sometimes the people on the outside of the walls are more broken than those on the inside.

I remember the first day I walked into this prison. I didn't know what to expect, but being inside a maximum-security prison made me feel different in a way I could never have imagined. In fact, I felt free.

～

The Louisiana State Penitentiary, or Angola as people like to call it, is special. It houses about sixty-three hundred inmates, 90 percent of whom are serving life sentences. It was given the nickname Angola because the land on which it is situated was once a plantation that served as a breeding ground for slaves taken from the Angola region of central Africa. Angolans were known to be larger than most Africans, and so Southern slave owners bred them as desirable field hands. But there's more.

Even after slavery was abolished in 1865, this plantation, which is now the size of Manhattan Island, continued to operate into the early 1900s. Finally, after the government caught wind of how much the plantation owners were profiting even after abolition, they forced the plantation to be turned into a prison. Still, this prison kept the workings of plantation life, with the continuation of convict labor on the inside and the strict state laws intent on returning former slaves back into bondage on the outside. Not much has changed since then. Louisiana is still one of the strictest states in the country when it comes to crime. Petty crimes often lead to life sentences with no chance of parole.

Hopeless people in hopeless situations tend to live recklessly. And that's how prisoners lived for years here. It was one of the most dangerous prisons in the world. Inmates raped each other, injured each other, and even killed each other. Corrections officers were fair game as well. It was not a place anyone wanted to be.

But then something happened. Burl Cain was named warden in 1995, and he changed everything. "Instead of treating these men like animals," he said, "we are going to treat them like human beings. These men need to know that they're loved. That there's hope outside these walls. Once they know that, everything will change."[4] Warden Cain bet big on this prison, and it paid off. It took eighteen years, but the Louisiana State Penitentiary went from being one of the most dangerous prisons on earth to one of the safest. Warden Cain implemented a mentorship program and paths to getting high school and college degrees while in prison. He even implemented a pastoral program in which inmates could become pastors. Today, there are twenty-seven inmate-led churches on the prison grounds. I have been to one of them, and it was amazing.

What I saw there on my first visit changed me. I saw men who were given opportunities. Men who were rehabilitated. Men who were loved. These men ministered to me in ways I never thought imaginable. They were following Christ with their whole hearts. I felt safe, surrounded by a group of men who looked and acted like men are supposed to act. Men who studied God's Word, kept each other accountable, and lived out the gospel.

One of my friends who was serving a life sentence actually transferred to a new prison to become a missionary. God doesn't waste anything, anyone, or any situation. So be you. Even if you're locked up in a prison cell, be you. God sees you. God knows you. God has great plans for you. Get to know Jesus intimately. Don't waste a second. He may be calling you to something greater.

> **God doesn't waste anything, anyone, or any situation. So be you.**

❦

My first experience at the Louisiana State Penitentiary was so impactful that I visited another prison as soon as I returned to Chicago. But my Cook County jail visit was much different. It was much like the Louisiana State

Penitentiary of old. It was one of the most dangerous places I ever saw.

During my visit to the Louisiana State Penitentiary, I went to death row and talked with some of the men there. It was peaceful. In fact, I did more listening than talking. Most of the guys on death row don't have anyone to talk to. They're locked in their cells for twenty-three hours a day. So when I came by they talked, and I listened. I heard many stories that day. But more testimonies than anything because these men on death row had encountered Jesus. Instead of me preaching to them, they were preaching to me. One man in particular was singing as I walked in. It was a song about the goodness of God. Another guy recited Scripture to me. He was rattling off verses from books of the Bible I had only skimmed. I was not afraid.

But the Cook County jail visit incited fear in me. I did not feel safe in the least. I could feel the demonic presence in that place. It was scary. Most of the people I met there weren't dangerous; it was the people I didn't meet. The guys they wouldn't let out of their cells that day. It was an eerie feeling. I was deep inside the walls of a very dangerous place.

God, however, continually reminded me, just as he did on the football field and as he would months and years later, "Do not fear, for I am with you" (Isa. 41:10). And I believed him. I had gotten to know Jesus a little better by then. I knew he wouldn't put me in a situation to harm me. I knew I was there for a reason. But I also knew I could not back down. When I spoke with the men there, I felt God's presence with me. I felt like a lion. I've felt this way a few times on the football field as well. It's how I know I'm walking in God's purpose for me. It's a feeling that something inside me, something that is greater than me, is at work. There's no better feeling. That is me. That is Christ within me, the hope of glory.

I spoke with conviction and power that day at the Cook County jail. I did not back down and did not mince words. God gave me a voice, and he wanted me to use it for his glory. I spoke with compassion as well. I told the men that there is a God who sees them, who knows them, and who loves them. A God who can change their situation from the inside out. A God who longs for them to know him. They listened with open ears, eager to hear about this Savior.

It's funny what happens when you are in a desperate situation. You pay a lot more attention to everything. The men at the Louisiana State Penitentiary and at Cook County jail knew they had a sin problem. They knew they needed help. For them it was easy to agree with Paul's tough but true words in Romans 3:23: "For all have sinned and fall short of the glory of God." And since they could not argue against how much they had sinned and fallen short, the impact of other passages in Scripture was that much more powerful:

But God demonstrates his own love for us in this: While we were still sinners, Christ died for us. (Rom. 5:8)

As far as the east is from the west, so far has he removed our transgressions from us. (Ps. 103:12)

He will never leave you nor forsake you. (Deut. 31:6)

Then you will call on me and come and pray to me, and I will listen to you. You will seek me and find me when you seek me with all your heart. (Jer. 29:12–13)

In prison, these men's lives had been changed because they made a decision that, no matter the circumstances, they were going to seek God wholeheartedly. And God showed up. He always does.

George showed up as well. He went with me on my second visit to the Louisiana State Penitentiary. By then I was family to the inmates there. I once left the group and got lost inside the prison walls. I was scared for a moment, but one of the inmates happily escorted me back to my group.

George saw what I saw. He saw men whose lives had been changed. Though he approached the situation with trepidation, he left forever changed. God showed up. George showed up too. I'm glad I have a friend like George.

## chapter eleven

# THE SUPER BOWL
# OF JUSTICE

During my nine years in the NFL, I experienced more losses than wins. Many of my seasons fell short of expectations, and I made it to the playoffs only twice, losing both games in the first round. I did, however, make it to the Super Bowl one year. Just not the way I expected.

The 2017 season with the Chicago Bears was tumultuous for me. Though I was experiencing success off the field with the growing relationship with ownership, my on-the-field play was struggling. And with my struggles on the field came doubt and anxiety, and sin was creeping up to the door, waiting to come in.

I did well in the first game of the season. I took a majority of the snaps and made a ton of plays against the defending NFC champions. Never had I received so many compliments from my coaches, teammates, and staff. I was on cloud nine, and I wanted to stay there.

People pleasing has always been a thing for me. I was keenly aware of the looks or the "look aways" people might give. I fed off the affirmation; I felt accepted and loved. But feelings aren't always based on reality, and most of the time those feelings of acceptance were based on my good (to them) performances. And that's where I fell into the trap. I performed and performed just to feel accepted, knowing deep down that this kind of acceptance wasn't based on *who* I was but how I *performed*. I figured if I performed better, I would eventually be fully accepted and fully loved. But 1 John 4:18 warns, "There is no fear in love, but perfect love casts out fear. For fear has to do with punishment, and whoever fears has not been perfected in love" (ESV). I was trying to receive perfect love from an imperfect place, as opposed to from a perfect Savior. I would find out the hard way that trying to receive perfect love from anyone but God never works.

I played great in our first game and felt loved, and I wanted more. So when game two arrived, my focus was no longer on playing my best but on what the coach would think of the plays I made. During the game, the opposing team ran a play that hurt us. While there was nothing I could have done differently to impact that particular play, all of a sudden fear crept in. I thought, *What are the coaches going to think I should have done? I need to do something to make it right.* A few plays later, I gambled on a play and abandoned my actual responsibility with the hope of being the hero and making a huge play. Well, I was wrong. I played more the fool than the hero. And our team paid for it. I tried again later in the game, thinking, *If I could just make a play like all these other guys, then the coach would really be impressed with me.*

I was wrong again. I was benched for the rest of that game and hardly played during the next two games. I was crushed. I started feeling angry and anxious. I was praying, but it was as if God wasn't hearing me. And then I had my eyes opened by a passage of Scripture.

⌣

There are certain passages that most Christians know by heart. Jeremiah 29:11 is one of these: "'For I know the plans I have for you,' declares the LORD, 'plans to prosper you and not to harm you, plans to give you hope and a future.'" This passage is a great encouragement to anyone going through tough times. It's a reminder of who God is and how he thinks about his people. But what's interesting here is who God was speaking to at the time.

God was speaking to the exiles, his chosen people who were displaced. They had been taken from their homes and were living as refugees in a foreign land. God was telling *them* that he was taking care of them. And he is telling us the same thing. But what's even more interesting than this verse that everyone focuses on are the verses that come before it.

In verse 7, God told the exiles, the refugees, the immigrants to "seek the welfare of the city where I have sent you into exile, and pray to the LORD on its behalf, for in its welfare you will find your welfare" (ESV).

That was huge for me. God was reminding me that I was in this city to do more than just play football. I was there to seek the welfare of the place he had sent me. And in its well-being I would be better off. This was bigger than sports, bigger than wins and losses, bigger than anyone's approval. God was already pleased with me, and he had good plans for me. I just needed to expand my vision.

〰

As the year progressed, I played better and better, but only after I started seeking the welfare of the city of Chicago. I spent my days off at homeless shelters, orphanages, schools, and after-school programs. I looked for as many ways as possible to provide hope to anyone who needed it. One of the benefits of being a professional athlete is that, for better or for worse, people listen to what you have to say. Doors were opened for me to share hope to hopeless people in hopeless situations. Children without parents. People without jobs, homes, or food. God gave me a platform, and it was time for me to use it. And God gave me favor.

I played well enough that season to receive some interest from other teams across the NFL. When free agency began, my agent told me a bidding war would ensue. I had heard so many stories about free agency, and now I would actually experience it firsthand. My desire was to stay in Chicago, but I also wanted to maximize this rare opportunity to be highly compensated for my performance. After a few days of negotiations, I received a multiyear, multimillion-dollar contract to stay in Chicago and be the starting outside linebacker. I had finally received the stability and security I had been looking for. I was finally the Man, and nothing was going to stop me from continuing my breakout performance. I thought I was going to set the league on fire, but God once again reminded me that his plans are much, much bigger than mine.

When the 2018 season opened, I was a starter. I was ready to channel my full energy into the season and into helping our team win a Super Bowl. Then all of a sudden the Bears traded for one of the best defensive players this generation has ever seen. And he happened to play my position.

Soccer has Lionel Messi and Cristiano Ronaldo.

Art has Salvador Dalí and Pablo Picasso.

Music has Wolfgang Amadeus Mozart.

And the NFL has Khalil Mack.

Khalil is often referred to as a generational talent, a once-in-a-lifetime type of player, and the best football player in the NFL, hands down. And now he was my teammate. But not only my teammate, he was the guy who was to come in and make the team better—by taking *my* spot.

I was not oblivious to replacements in football, but I was still frustrated. I had done everything in my power to play well the year before, and I was told by the coaches and by the contract I signed that it was enough, that *I* was enough. And then I wasn't.

I searched for a silver lining. But week after week, after playing less and less in the games and participating less and less in practice, I began to pray. *God, I don't know what you're doing, but make it clear what your plans are for me. You know me, you made me, you know my desires. Just open up a door.* And he did. Just not the way I was thinking.

A few days later, on a routine play, I tore my pectoral muscle and was out for the rest of season. It's funny, because during that time the NFL had a huge social justice initiative going on that I was really excited about. But because of the time required for practice, games, and meetings, I couldn't be as involved as I wanted. And I wanted to do more to help the city of Chicago. I wanted to suffer with the city and gain a better understanding of the causes of some of the violence. I wanted to seek the welfare of the place God had placed me. This was my desire. It's what I was created to do.

As they say, be careful what you wish for, because you just might get it.

Though I was injured, I felt a huge sigh of relief. God had answered my prayer. So a few days later, after a bit of mourning, I went deeper into a journey that had begun a few months earlier.

In response to the social justice discussion that began with Colin Kaepernick's national anthem protest, the NFL started a financial matching program designed to find solutions to the problems players were seeing in their communities. The league office decided that if the players were serious about changing their communities, then the NFL as a collective body would support the players to the tune of $250,000 per year per team. If the players gave money to an organization to fight injustice, their teams would have to give to the organization as well. But there was a catch. The league only required the teams to *match* what the players raised. And this is where I saw an opportunity.

I love rallying people together, creating relationships, and building things. Before the season began, I saw a perfect opportunity to do this.

The Bears happened to play in the first preseason and the first regular season games that year, so we would be the first team on national television one season after the protests began. Once again, all eyes would be on us.

Meanwhile, the NFL had recently made a rule that players were not allowed to kneel during the anthem. Players were allowed to stay in the locker room during the pregame events, but if they came out onto the field, they would have to stand for the anthem with their hands over their hearts or be fined. Though this rule was quickly rescinded, no one knew how the players were going to respond when the preseason began.

For our part, my teammates and I wanted to be united, but we also wanted to be strategic. And thanks to some good friends, we did both.

We decided to lock arms again that year, but we knew that wouldn't be enough. When we heard about the matching grant program, we wanted to be the first team to max out the allotted money. I saw the matching grant as a dare. Some owners didn't think the players cared enough about social justice to put their money where their mouths were, and I wanted to prove them wrong. We all did.

So the night before that first preseason game, five of us came up with a plan to meet the $250,000 limit.

Tight end Trey Burton said, "So that's $25,000 from ten players. That shouldn't be too difficult."

I had my doubts, but Trey didn't.

Trey was a follower of Christ who had just come off a career high. As a player for the Philadelphia Eagles, he had just won the Super Bowl and had thrown the game-winning score, which would later be nominated for Best Play at the ESPYs. He was also coming off another high because his former team was making major headway spiritually. Guys were being baptized, disciples were being made, and a city was being changed. Before the Bears offered me the contract I eventually signed, I hoped I would wind up in Philly. Instead, God brought Philly to me.

Trey and I immediately hit it off. I knew something of his character based on some mutual friends, but what I didn't know was that he was exactly who I needed in my life that season.

Has God ever put people in your life exactly when you needed them? Has he ever given you a friend for the perfect season? Someone who had your back when no one else would? God did that for me.

I was reminded of David and Jonathan's friendship (1 Sam. 20). David had just defeated Goliath and was already chosen by God to be the next king, although Jonathan was the king's son and the next in line. Things started off fine, but then King Saul started to feel jealous of David after hearing of David's successes in war. Saul became very angry to the point where

> Has God ever put people in your life exactly when you needed them? . . . God did that for me.

he wanted to kill David. When Jonathan heard about his father's plan, he warned David. He saved David's life. He loved him like a brother. Saul and Jonathan later died in battle, and David became king.

You need good friends. We all do.

During one of his first weeks in Chicago, Trey and I met up at a barbecue place and shared our dreams for the city. We envisioned a better Chicago and wondered if God had brought us together to do something about the problems we saw. Our personalities couldn't have been more different, but our combined strengths couldn't have been more perfect. I am eccentric, excitable, and a starter. Trey is calm, measured, and a finisher. I talk about big dreams and big ideas. Trey talks about practical plans and steps to accomplish those goals. We were a perfect match. So when I approached Trey with a crazy idea for raising the $250,000, he came back with a practical plan.

Trey already knew what I was about to find out: many people with wealth are generous, but sometimes they need a push. His plan was simple. Start with the guys on the team who made over a certain amount. Explain our vision to them, and ask if they would contribute to the cause. He figured if we got seven or so guys to commit to giving $25,000, the rest would be easy. But we had to start with the big-money guys first. And for the first time in my career, I was a part of that list.

My previous contracts always placed me toward the

bottom of the league. I had a rookie contract with the Cardinals that was pegged at the minimum salary, and I had signed three consecutive one-year veteran minimum contracts with the Bears. Many people think all professional athletes are millionaires, but that's not true. Though I had been making great money, it was next to nothing compared to my fourth-year contract with the Bears.

That year was the first year I had some movement in free agency. I had finally learned to be me and not care about people's opinions, and it really paid off. I played well, and teams showed interest. I actually ended up staying with Chicago after receiving a miracle contract for $3 million for one year. I say "miracle" because most guys my age and in my position are usually out of the NFL. I also say it because I agreed to the contract while I was visiting the maximum-security prison with George McCaskey.

I'll never forget my agent's reaction when he found out where I was and who I was with. "You're *with* the owner right now?!" he exclaimed. "Dude, put some pressure on him. Tell him about the other offers you have on the table and how you're willing to leave. A little nudge couldn't hurt!"

But I refused. George was my friend, and I was tired of meddling with God's plans. If God wanted me in Chicago, he would have to do it on his terms, not mine.

The night before, I had prayed. I told God my exact request. Then I went to sleep. I woke up the next morning and went to the prison focused on spending time with my friends. I encouraged them, they encouraged me, and then my phone rang. The Chicago Bears were offering me the exact amount I had been praying for and felt I deserved. I said yes.

No one was happier in that moment than George. He didn't know the status of the negotiations. He liked to stay out of the football business and refused to be involved with any player negotiations; he left that to the *football* people. George knew who he was and who he wasn't. When he saw the news that I had signed, he ran from the back of the prison to the front steps to give me a hug. He was happy for me. I was happy too. God had done it.

When Trey and I discussed our strategy for raising the social justice money, I committed to become one of the guys who would make this dream of change a reality. That night six other guys committed to support the cause as well. In the coming weeks forty-four of the fifty-three guys on the team pledged to give something. Guys gave what they could, $30 for some and $30,000 for others. Not only did we meet our goal, but we exceeded it.

During the planning, Trey had heard about some other matching grants that either the team or the league had, and we decided to maximize those as well. Trey made the plans, I made the requests, and together we made a big change. Altogether we raised over $827,000 from the Bears players, coaches, and staff. And that money went to five organizations I had researched in depth after my injury in early October. We met with them and members of the University of Chicago Crime Lab to learn more about some of the issues and find ways we could help. Guys gave money, time, energy, advice, and facilities to see the city thrive. And when the city thrived, the team thrived. We had our best year in a decade and made the playoffs with one of the top defenses in the league.

Though we didn't go to the Super Bowl that year, the NFL featured me and a few of my teammates in the NFL Inspire Change commercial, which aired before, during, and after the Super Bowl. It may even still be showing today.

—

I decided not to resent the injury but to make the most of the opportunity. I became a friend to my teammates, a friend they all needed, and I just loved on them. I provided words of encouragement when guys were down. I sat with guys when they were injured. I celebrated their successes and mourned with their failures. I was me. And the world was a better place because of it.

For a guy who was always looking for love and recognition, I got more of that when I decided to stop pretending and start being the person God made me to be: a good friend, a lover of people, an evangelist, a child of God, a great host. Be you. It will pay off *big*. God will get the glory, the people around you will benefit, and the world around you will thrive. You'll feel a freedom that you've never experienced before. A freedom that comes from knowing you are loved *perfectly* by a perfect God. He is perfect so you don't have to be. He is the hero, not you. The story is about him.

Later that year I threw another party for my friends, the Third Annual Sam Acho Celebrity Waiter Night. By God's grace we raised almost $200,000, nearly triple what we had raised in prior years. God received the glory.

**Be you. It will pay off *big*.**

Get to know Jesus intimately and be you. The world is waiting.

## chapter twelve

# BLESSING

Our stories span generations. They span cultures, eras, people groups, and societies. Our stories are bigger than us, whether or not we actually believe it. I didn't think much about the breadth of my story until I met my wife.

My parents were born and raised in Nigeria. They immigrated to the United States when they were in their early twenties. The goal was to live a better life and to leave a legacy for their children. But they never forgot their roots. I was born in Dallas, Texas, but I have spent every other Christmas in Nigeria.

Christmas in Nigeria is very different. It's a weeklong celebration that begins on Christmas Eve and lasts until New Year's Day. I think that's where I learned to love good get-togethers. Each day you go to a different friend's house and celebrate with them. They welcome you into their home and you invite them into yours. You sit, you fellowship, you dance, you feast. Every day is a party.

Culturally, Nigeria is very different as well. Family relations are of the utmost importance. Children are an extension of their parents, even into adulthood. Culture, values, and family names are passed from generation to generation with the expectation that they will be kept in high esteem.

As a second-generation Nigerian American, I grew up in a mix of many worlds. Since I was good at sports, some people thought I was a dumb jock. I enjoyed school, so others thought I was a nerd. (They may have been right about that one.) I was a pastor's kid who knew Scripture and led Bible studies, so my friends thought I was perfect, but I was far from it. I lived in this universe of competing worlds with many competing value systems. My teammates thought I spent too much time on schoolwork. My classmates thought I spent too much time on sports. My peers thought I was too perfect. My parents were proud of the positive reports they received from everyone about their son. My coaches thought I could be more aggressive on the field. My friends thought I was too physical. I was a little kid in a big man's body and didn't know how to handle it.

I always felt like I was never enough. Not mean enough, not tough enough, not savvy enough. Just not enough, period. So whenever I met a situation that was too hard to handle, in crept doubt, fear, and anxiety. But by the grace of God, he provided me with someone who believed in me, even when I didn't believe in myself. But how he would do it was a surprise to both me and everyone around me.

Ngozi and I met when we were fifteen years old. She was living in Nigeria and I was visiting. I say I was visiting but this trip was different. Every summer my parents traveled to Nigeria to do medical mission work. And though I went with them to Nigeria for Christmas, I was never old enough to travel with them on the medical mission trips. That is, until I was fifteen. My joining them was a rite of passage. The things they saw on these trips could sometimes be jarring emotionally, mentally, and spiritually. But when I turned fifteen, my parents believed I was old enough to cope with the experience.

We were staying in the house my father had built in the village where his father had grown up. I think he wanted to build a place big enough for his large family and nice enough so his children would want to visit. Before he built the house, we stayed at my grandmother's hut. That's right, hut. The only light we had was a kerosene oil lamp. If anyone needed to "ease" themselves, there was a small shed out back with a hole in the ground. Still, that place was beautiful.

When my father came to America, God showed him favor. He worked, went to school, raised kids, and pastored a church. He became a marriage counselor and an entrepreneur, and God blessed his business. With the overflow, he built a large house in his family's Nigerian village, dug a well, and bought a generator. In the end, the home that he built for his family became a place that housed all the missionaries who came with him to Nigeria.

One day I was sitting in the living room, resting from a long day's work in the field, when I heard the unthinkable.

"Sam," Ms. Alys said, "you're gonna make a great husband one day. And, who knows, the woman of your dreams might be right under this very roof."

I didn't know what she was talking about.

Ms. Alys was a sixty-eight-year-old black woman from Dallas. And after watching how hard I worked, she saw something in me that I didn't see in myself. She saw someone's husband, someone's father, someone who loved Nigeria, someone after God's heart.

I saw none of that.

"Ms. Alys," I quipped. "You know we're in Nigeria, right? In the middle of a village."

I didn't know what had gotten into her. No one who accompanied us on that mission trip was even remotely near my age. Plus, I was only fifteen. How could she possibly know what kind of husband I would be?

I soon found out that older people often know much more than we can imagine. They have watched people and experienced life in ways that only time can allow. In fact, Ms. Alys knew *exactly* what she was talking about. And she could not have been more spot on. Because as she was talking to me, a fifteen-year-old Nigerian girl named Ngozi passed by the house. And many years later Ngozi would become my wife.

*Meek, humble,* and *servant* aren't words that US society places a high value on. As a matter of fact, our society seems to place a premium on the opposite qualities. Being aggressive, prideful, and self-centered are usually, one way or another, praiseworthy to most. But Jesus thought differently. To a crowd that was following him, he said:

> Blessed are the poor in spirit, for theirs is the kingdom
> of heaven.
> Blessed are those who mourn, for they shall be
> comforted.
> Blessed are the meek, for they shall inherit the earth.
> Blessed are those who hunger and thirst for
> righteousness, for they shall be satisfied.
> Blessed are the merciful, for they shall receive mercy.
> Blessed are the pure in heart, for they shall see God.
> Blessed are the peacemakers, for they shall be called
> sons of God.
> Blessed are those who are persecuted for righteousness'
> sake, for theirs is the kingdom of heaven.
> Blessed are you when others revile you and persecute
> you and utter all kinds of evil against you falsely
> on my account. Rejoice and be glad, for your
> reward is great in heaven, for so they persecuted
> the prophets who were before you.
> (Matt. 5:3–12 ESV)

Ngozi possessed all the qualities Jesus described as being blessed. So I guess it's of no surprise that her name, in our native dialect, means "blessing." God knew what he was doing.

Ngozi had moved to the village a few months before I was there for my first medical mission trip. Her father had died when she was two years old, leaving her mom and six young children behind. Nigeria is about family, so some of her family stepped in to help. Different siblings went to stay with different family members, and Ngozi and her twin brother were left in the care of an aunt in the city of Jos.

Jos, for those who are geographically inclined, is smack-dab in the middle of Nigeria. Why this is important is because the northern parts of Nigeria are predominately Muslim while the southern parts are predominately Christian. And so wars, strife, and violence occurred in the middle—that is, in Jos.

While Ngozi and her brother were at school, a bomb detonated in the streets. In the aftermath of the bombing, no one knew where the children were. Ngozi's mother frantically called her sister, trying to find her children. No one answered.

By God's grace they were okay, but enough was enough. Ngozi's mother demanded that her kids come home immediately. She didn't have much, but they were going to figure it out.

And God opened a door.

❦

My dad was in need. His mother, my grandmother and the matriarch of the family, was getting older. She had gotten sick and needed someone to take care of her, someone she could trust. The last young girl who had stayed with her was caught stealing, so my grandmother fired her. She was the seventh person she had fired for one reason or another. My grandmother is a no-nonsense woman. She didn't tolerate liars, cheaters, or prideful people. She was also pretty stubborn herself, so people didn't always put up with her. But she needed help. My dad called a friend, Ngozi's mother, to ask if she knew anyone. And she said she knew the perfect person for the job.

Imagine being fifteen years old, living in a city, making friends, going to school, going to church, living life, and then being told to move to a small village to take care of an elderly woman you didn't know. That's hard. But Ngozi's tough herself, so she said yes.

What was supposed to be a short-term job for a few weeks turned into a few months and then a few years. Ngozi learned to overlook little offenses and was glad to serve. It's who she is. She and my grandmother became bosom buddies and were nearly inseparable. Ngozi cooked for her, cleaned for her, and cared for her. She came close when others were running away. She had no expectations. She was just herself. And God honored that.

Sometimes God does things we will never understand. He puts us or people around us in situations that jar us, shake us, move us. What we fail to realize is that God is doing these things for our own good.

Every summer after I turned fifteen, I went to Nigeria and served on my parents' mission trips. It was what my family did. We served. And who did I see serving as well? Ngozi. It took me years to muster up the courage to say something to her. She was quiet, and I was confused. I knew God had placed her in my life for a reason, but I was struggling with my own identity issues. I loved Nigeria, loved the culture, and loved Ngozi, but I was too scared and confused to say anything. That is, until years later, when I received a not-so-gentle shove from one of my three-hundred-pound friends.

〜

Calais Campbell knows me well. Since the time I reached out to him after the draft through Twitter to ask if I could work out with him, he has been my best friend. He knows everything about me. My ins and outs, my likes and dislikes, even my favorite pass-rush moves. He trusts me. So when I invited him to Nigeria to join me on a medical mission trip, he obliged.

Calais had never been to Nigeria before. Actually, he had never even been out of the country. It took a huge leap of faith for him to make that trip. But that's who Calais is; he's a risk-taker.

The locals affectionately called him Goliath, and he is huge. He is six feet eight, three-hundred-plus pounds, and a lover of people. He has a brilliant smile that can light up a room and a booming voice that can tear it down. We had just gotten off the plane and walked out of the airport when he saw Ngozi for the first time.

"Bro, who is that?" he said. "Are y'all related?"

I was confused. Calais had just finished telling me about a girl he had recently started dating, a woman he claimed to be in love with. Why was he asking about Ngozi? I looked at him perplexed.

"No, bro," he explained. "I'm not asking for my sake. I'm asking for yours. She is everything you always talked about *and* more!"

The interesting thing is that I had never talked to Calais about Ngozi. He just knew me. He had worked with me, played with me, and now he was serving with me. He knew me inside and out, so when he saw Ngozi, he gave me a push.

Sometimes God puts people like Calais in our lives. People who know us fully. People who can help us make better decisions. Proverbs 11:14 says, "For lack of guidance a nation falls, but victory is won through many advisers." Well, I had a good adviser in Calais. A mentor really.

Calais encouraged me to have a conversation with Ngozi that summer. And his encouragement on that day was the reason he'd return to Nigeria the next summer.

Even after that initial push from Calais, it still took me a few days to muster up the courage to say anything. Thankfully, as I was being me, God spoke. This time through some kids.

A few days into the trip, I was playing with some young-sters. I love kids. I'm a big kid myself, so I can relate. As we were outside playing, one of the girls saw Ngozi walk by and asked, "Wow, who is that? She's beautiful. Is that your wife?"

I was starting to get the message. First Ms. Alys, then Calais, now this young girl. I would love to say I went right over to Ngozi and proposed then and there, but that's not what happened. I was with two little helpers, so I called Ngozi over and started a conversation. I told her what they had said. She laughed, asking them if they even knew what marriage was. We talked a little longer, but then she went back to work.

I was still too scared to say anything, and chances are I always would have been. Thankfully, Ngozi isn't like me. That night she couldn't sleep and she knew why. Even better, the next day she was brave enough to do something about it.

Ngozi follows God wholeheartedly. She had been praying for a husband and had already had many people ask for her hand in marriage. But none of them seemed right. The next morning, I heard a knock on my door. It was Ngozi.

She was doing the routine wake-up calls for all the missionaries. Except this wake-up call wasn't so routine.

I opened the door.

"Just letting you know that breakfast and morning devotion will start in thirty minutes," she began.

"Okay," I replied, surprised that she was the one doing the wake-up calls that morning because it wasn't normally her responsibility.

But before I could close the door, she said, "Oh, by the way, I would love to talk with you sometime today when you get the chance."

I nodded and gave a sheepish, "Okay."

I was shocked, surprised, confused, and alarmed. I had a million different emotions turning inside me and didn't know what to think. Thankfully, my teammate and roommate Calais was there with me.

"Ooh, she likes you!" he said in jest as she closed the door.

I told him to quiet down.

Later that day, while on break from work, I called Ngozi into a side room and we talked. She told me she couldn't shake what those girls had said the day before and wanted to at least have a conversation with me. We discovered we had a lot in common. Right before we left, she said, "I think we should pray." And pray we did.

Eleven months later we celebrated our traditional Nigerian wedding, with Calais Campbell and over two thousand people from surrounding villages. Like I said, Nigerians know how to party.

The marriage process in America is straightforward. You start dating, meet the parents, ask the dad for his daughter's hand in marriage, propose, and then get married. It is much different in Nigeria.

The first step in the process is called *ekoaka* ("knocking on the door"). This is the official introduction you make to the woman you want to marry. After that is an investigatory period in which the families ask the community about each other and the kind of people the man and the woman are. Then comes the *ipaugba* ("bride price"). This is money or things you give your soon-to-be wife's mother, family, and community to show them appreciation for raising her. Goats, yams, soaps, lotions, underwear, and suitcases were some of the items on the list I was given. Our engagement was an amazing experience. It was her and me. Two cultures coming together to create something greater.

On the day of our wedding, Calais asked me, "Has this been the best day ever?"

"I don't know yet," I responded. "Ask me when the day is over."

He did. And my answer was yes.

God changed my life that day. He introduced me to a woman who knew more about me than I knew about myself. She knew about my family. She knew stories about my dad that even I had never heard. She knew about my community, my heritage. She knew me. How? Because she knew the people who knew me best.

━

In the years that followed, Ngozi has come to know me even better, and I her. We have gotten to know each other intimately. She's seen me at my highs and my lows, my injuries and my inking million-dollar contracts. She's seen my sins and my successes, my failures and my fallbacks. And she still loves me. God loves us the same way, except his love is immeasurably greater. I think Paul said it best in Ephesians 3:18–20:

> I pray that you and all God's holy people will have the power to understand the greatness of Christ's love. I pray that you can understand how wide and how long and how high and how deep that love is. Christ's love is greater than any person can ever know. But I pray that you will be able to know that love. Then you can be filled with the fullness of God.
>
> With God's power working in us, God can do much, much more than anything we can ask or think of. (ICB)

God did much more than I ever imagined in giving me a wife. As it says in Proverbs 19:14, "Houses and wealth are inherited from parents, but a prudent wife is from the LORD." God knew me. And he put people around me who would help me get to know myself better.

Get to know Jesus intimately. He will show you how much you are loved.

## chapter thirteen

# THE ART OF THE PIVOT

Life is about growth. Life is about transition. But one of the most difficult things in life is learning how to transition well.

Everyone who has been around children knows they grow through phases. They lie on their backs for a while, and then they begin to sit up. After sitting up for a while, they begin to crawl. After crawling for a while, they take their first steps. These baby steps are a huge accomplishment. But they are not the end goal. Babies and kids are not meant to stop growing. They are meant to keep on walking, running, jumping, falling, and getting up again and again. Children are meant to grow, to share, to learn, to create, and to teach others.

Adults aren't meant to stop growing either. Whatever you may have placed your identity in, it could very well be just another baby step in your growth.

Playing in the NFL was a baby step for me. It was a

huge accomplishment to play professionally for nine years. Millions of kids dream about this opportunity and work toward it their whole lives. But once you make it, it is nearly impossible for it *not* to become your identity. It's like that with most jobs, successes, family ties, and other things in which we put our identity.

In sports, and basketball in particular, there's something called a pivot. A pivot is when you have one foot down and can advance your position without changing your location. People who can master the pivot in sports drastically increase their chances for success. Life is no different. In life, you have to be fully committed to be where you are while maintaining the ability to pivot, to change direction, to do something different. Those who can do this well are on their way to achieving success during life's downturns.

In finance, investors call it diversifying your portfolio. I call it mastering the pivot. It means starting to do some of the things you *want* to do while doing whatever you *have* to do. With any job, there will be times—mornings, evenings, weekends, holidays—when you get to explore. These are times when you can begin to prioritize learning how to pivot.

Two separate times during my career I had major season-ending injuries. During these times I was sad, sure, but I learned to look at the time off as an opportunity. An opportunity to explore some of the things I enjoyed doing since my main job was temporarily on hold. While doing my best to pivot during these times, I learned four key principles that helped me along the way. I believe they are both crucial and applicable to anyone looking to make a transition.

**1. Find your limitation and work around it.** In 2013, I was out for the season with a broken leg. I knew I would be limited as far as movement went because I would be in a cast. I also knew I would have to start rehab soon, from 8:00 a.m. to noon every weekday. This meant my afternoons were available. I didn't want to be alone, so I decided to share my experience with other people who were going through pain as I was. I wanted to go to homeless shelters and schools for kids with autism. I wanted to check out orphanages and boys' and girls' homes. I also had an interest in being on television, so I called a local station, told them what I planned to do, and asked if they wanted to send a camera. They said yes.

So every Tuesday, after rehab, I drove to one of these places, met the cameraman, and loved on people. And I loved it. I was pretty good at it too. I was so good that the station started a weekly segment called "Sam in the City."

**2. Push yourself, and don't be afraid to ask.** The second important factor in learning how to pivot is knowing how to push yourself. The fifteen-minute weekly television segment was fun, but I wanted to try something more difficult. I wanted to see if I could host the news. After seeing me in action for a few months, the station obliged. For a week I hosted the Channel 12 news in Phoenix. It was fun, but it wasn't my thing. I never would have known that if I hadn't given it a shot.

After that week of hosting the news, I wanted to see if I

could host my own show. It had been one of my desires for a while, so I prayed about it and asked God to open a door. He did. A few weeks later, one of the producers approached me with an idea for a show. I said yes. The next year, after recovering from the injury and getting back on the field, I hosted a weekly show called, you guessed it, *The Sam Acho Show*. I interviewed local celebrities, talked about issues I was passionate about, and played games with kids. I had a blast.

Though I was still rehabbing and training, I knew that football wouldn't last forever. I was testing the waters and touching doorknobs to see if there was anything else I liked to do. There was. And thus I gained a little more information about who I was when that transition from player to something else came. I also developed relationships and built bridges with people I cared about and who cared about me. I took some risks and they were well worth it.

**3. Serve others.** Learning what you love doesn't always have to be about you. One place to start is serving others. A marketing professor in college taught a concept that has stuck with me: find a need and fill it. To properly pivot, you have to be aware of other people's needs.

In 2018, I tore a pectoral muscle. This injury was different from my previous injury because many things in my life had changed. This time I had a wife and three kids at home, and I no longer had a desire to leave them regularly to film anything for television. But I had a desire to serve my teammates. I had noticed, in my eight years of playing, that many professional athletes, CEOs, and pastors have a lot of people who want something from them, but they rarely have any real friends. People they could count on and people who could count on them. After all, friendship is a two-way street. So I stopped focusing on myself and started looking for ways to serve others.

Though I was injured and my rehab didn't start until later in the day, I showed up early at the team facilities and helped lead our team Bible study. There were a few guys interested in learning more about God, and many of us seemed to be going through similar temptations, doubts, and fears. So I figured that sacrificing thirty minutes a day to meet together and grow together would be worth it. It was. We grew spiritually and had a better understanding of how God wanted us to conduct our lives based on Scripture. We leaned on each other during our difficult times and celebrated our successes together. And God always showed up.

Another way I served my teammates was by simply listening to them. People are constantly on the go in our culture. We move so fast we don't pay attention to what we're feeling. I would just sit with a teammate and listen. Often that was enough to let my teammates know they were cared about and loved. That time together helped me too. One thing I deeply desire is relationship. We are all created for it, but I've got some extra receptacles in my tank. I need people. So by serving people, I was serving myself too.

Though I didn't receive any monetary reward from these actions, I gained more than I could have ever imagined.

I gave my life away, and by doing so I saw something remarkable. I saw people grow physically, emotionally, and spiritually in ways I hadn't seen in years. Because I was no longer as focused on myself, I was able to truly serve the needs of others. Everyone benefitted. I learned more about who I was, and my teammates received a healthier, less self-centered version of me.

**4. Don't forget to mourn.** Lastly, whenever you go through a transition, you have to be okay with the mourning process. Losing something is hard. Whether it's a job, a relationship, or a loved one, nobody likes experiencing loss. But loss is a part of life. There's no way around it. Solomon said it best in Ecclesiastes 3:1–4:

> For everything there is a season, and a time for every matter under heaven: a time to be born, and a time to die; a time to plant, and a time to pluck up what is planted; a time to kill, and a time to heal; a time to break down, and a time to build up; a time to weep, and a time to laugh; a time to mourn, and a time to dance. (ESV)

There is a time for *everything*, including mourning. Many of us, including me, don't like to read about that truth. And even if we read it, we definitely don't believe it.

Mourning is for the weak, we think. We say to ourselves, *Real men don't cry; that's for children.* But thoughts like that couldn't be further from the truth. Real men *and* real women cry. They mourn, they grieve, they lament. These emotions—mourning, grief, regret—bring healing. But if we

THE ART OF THE PIVOT

never address our pain, how can we heal? The answer is that we can't.

That's what Justice Alan Page realized all those years ago when he decided to address America's ugly past. He was after hope. He was after healing. We live in a generation full of broken, hurting people. People who refuse to trust God with their sadness. To trust him with their pain.

I recently went through a really tough time. While finishing this book, I lost a very close family member. It was and still is tough. Harder than I could have imagined. And to be honest, I didn't want to mourn. I didn't want to cry. But as I read back some of this writing, I was reminded of an extremely difficult truth: I must mourn if I want to heal. I cannot run from pain. I cannot hide from sadness. It's time for me to let the world see me. Teardrops and all.

These four lessons became great guides for me as I prepared for what was about to come.

●

For me, 2018 was a tumultuous year. From January to December things didn't seem to be going my way. The year began with a car accident in January and ended with the loss of a loved one in December. And much more loss happened in between. I'm learning that loss is a part of life.

I lost my car in January. I knew the brakes were in need of some attention, but I had been putting off getting them fixed for a while. The season had just ended, and I had a flight out that day. I was driving up to the practice facility one last time before leaving Chicago for the off-season. It was snowing, the roads were icy, and quite frankly, I was driving too fast. As I pulled into the gate, I tried to slow down and allow the attendant to open the gate, but my speed, along with the patch of black ice on the road, didn't allow that to happen. I skidded down the road and ran into a pole protecting the sensor that allowed vehicles access. My airbags inflated and, at the same time, my ego deflated. My car was totaled. People compare the impact of football games to mini-accidents. Well, now I can tell you, they're right. This was not the way I wanted to start off the year, but it would most definitely be a sign of things to come.

In August I was at Highland Park Hospital for the birth of our third child. Our baby was born around noon, and it seemed as if everything was going well. We named him Kelechi, which means "Thank God" in Igbo, because we had so much to be thankful for. A little after the birth of our son, Ngozi complained to the doctors about some pain in her stomach. My wife is not one to complain, but the doctors didn't know that, and they didn't take it seriously. Twelve hours later, the pain had become excruciating. So much so that I woke up in the middle of the night to a roomful of nurses and my wife screaming. I had seen nurses rush to a patient's room during some of my prior visits, but I had never actually been *inside* the room when it happened. Now, not only was I in the room, but I was directly impacted by the situation.

I didn't know what was going on. Ngozi had just had her third C-section, and the doctors were taking her away for another surgery. They left me with our twelve-hour-old child. I was scared. I remember both crying and *crying out* to God. I told him I hadn't signed up for this. It wasn't part of our agreement. I begged him, pleaded with him to save Ngozi's life.

*You're the same God yesterday, today, and forever.*
*You're the same God who raised Lazarus from the*
*dead, the same God who spoke to the wind and the*
*waves and calmed the storm. You did it before. You*
*can do it again. Just say the word. Just say the word.*
*Just say the word!*

I was an emotional wreck. I reminded God of his promises and of his power. I know God doesn't need our reminders, but they definitely don't hurt.

*The wind and the waves listen to your voice, Lord.*
*The trees obey you. All creation listens to you, God.*
*So speak. Speak to this situation. Say the word and*
*she will be healed. Say the word.*

As I was crying out, I felt a whisper in my spirit: *She's healed.*

*Good,* I responded.

Kelechi, my newborn son, and I listened to music and waited. Hours passed. I was determined to stay awake until Ngozi came back, but I couldn't. I woke up a few hours later to use the restroom, and as I was walking back, I saw the nurses wheeling Ngozi back into the room. It turned out she was suffering from blood clots that were too big to safely pass through, so they had to perform an emergency surgery to remove them. This was her third C-section and another big baby—ten pounds, seven ounces to be exact. He was born a few weeks early as well.

God had healed my wife, but unfortunately that was not the end of our difficult 2018.

When was the last time you cried out to God? The last time you pleaded with him? I'm talking the kind of pleading like we find in Psalm 55:1–2: "Give ear to my prayer, O God, and hide not yourself from my plea for mercy! Attend to me, and answer me; I am restless in my complaint and I moan" (ESV).

God hears our requests. He hears our prayers. He shows compassion toward his creation. Even if we don't see it. Don't wait until you're in a desperate situation. Cry out to God. Let him know your requests, your needs, your issues. He hears your prayers.

> Don't wait until you're in a desperate situation. Cry out to God. . . . He hears your prayers.

After Ngozi's surgery I returned to training camp. Two weeks later I lost my starting position when the team traded for Khalil Mack. Two weeks after that I tore my pec and was out for the season. Two months after the injury I lost my friend Jerry Price, my old neighbor and mentor and the inspiration for this book. Certainly, things had to start to turn around, don't you think? They didn't.

The following month a pipe burst in our house, causing it to flood and my family and me to move out. Three weeks later I was released by the Bears, just one year into a two-year deal.

Have you ever been in a season of life when things didn't

go right? In 2018, and into part of 2019, it seemed as if there were failures and disappointments at every turn. Well, I'm here to tell you that those failures and disappointments are not the end of the story. And here's why.

There's a concept known as failing forward. It means there's a silver lining in the mistakes, in the changes, in the uncertainties of life. You're not losing; you're learning. Learning to rely on Jesus. Though it was hard, I learned so much about myself during this season of my life. I learned I didn't need all the things I thought I needed to be happy. All I needed was Jesus. Period. I lost my car, my house, my job, my friend, my stability. But Jesus gave me something far more precious in the meantime. He gave me his presence. He gave me his peace. He showed me that nothing can separate me from his love. During this time, God taught me the real comforts of his everlasting love.

> What then shall we say to these things? If God is for us, who can be against us? . . . Who shall separate us from the love of Christ? Shall tribulation, or distress, or persecution, or famine, or nakedness, or danger, or sword? . . .
>
> No, in all these things we are more than conquerors through him who loved us. For I am sure that neither death nor life, nor angels nor rulers, nor things present nor things to come, nor powers, nor height nor depth, nor anything else in all creation, will be able to separate us from the love of God in Christ Jesus our Lord. (Rom. 8:31, 35, 37–39 ESV)

God is good. We are loved.

Recently I had a discussion with God. I was sad, angry, lost, and confused. I wanted to run from God. I tried to run from him, but he tracked me down. I found myself flat on my face in prayer, asking if he would still love me in the midst of my brokenness.

*There's no way you still love me after this mistake. I'm sorry I ran from you.*

But God's reminders are greater than our remarks. And just like all those times before, I heard it. That still, small voice. And what I heard was stern but simple: *You don't get to decide how much I love you. That's not your call to make. I decide. Not you. Don't you dare forget it.*

Point taken. And I want to remind you, wherever you are reading these words, there is *nothing* that can separate you from the love of God. Not even your mistakes.

When you lose, you win. That's how it works in God's economy. Jesus told his disciples, "But your sorrow will turn into joy. When a woman is giving birth, she has sorrow because her hour has come, but when she has delivered the baby, she no longer remembers the anguish, for joy that a human being has been born into the world" (John 16:20–21 ESV).

If you're reading this and you don't believe this is true, it's time to start believing. Things may seem like they're hopeless, but they're not. You are being made new. These are just the growing pains. This is just a phase. You are loved. Loved by a good, good God. You are chosen. You are his. Nothing can separate you from his love.

Transition can be hard. But it doesn't have to be. We can make it easier by learning to pivot. There will be mourning and there will be testing. There will be doubt and there will be fear. But do not be afraid. These are all normal parts of the transition. You'll get to the other side. It will just take some time.

## chapter fourteen

# IN THE BEGINNING

We all need people to inspire us. To push us. To encourage us. To be honest with us. To hold us accountable. To know who we are and to remind us of who that is. To tell us the truth no matter what. To see us and make sure we let the world see us. These people are called mentors. We all need them in our lives. I know I do. A mentor is part of the reason I made it to the NFL.

When I was growing up, I never desired to play football for a living. I honestly didn't even like watching it on television. Many of my Saturday afternoons were spent watching cartoons, not college football. That's why it's so surprising I ended up where I am today. That said, I did play sports at a young age. My parents thought it was a good way for my brother and me to release some of our energy and not break things in the house. Soccer, basketball, and baseball were the first sports I played. Later, after seeing my younger brother play football and score touchdowns—and hearing the cheers that followed—my desire to play the game grew. The only problem was that no one was cheering me on because playing my position well meant no one ever heard my name.

I played on the offensive line. As an offensive lineman, your job is to be unnoticed. You protect the quarterback and allow him to make the plays. You block for the running backs and help them score all the touchdowns. The only time your name gets called is if you make a mistake and have a penalty. I hated this about my position.

Proverbs 29:25 says, "The fear of man brings a snare" (NKJV). And my fear was not being seen. Not being known. For the longest time, recognition was very important to me. I wanted my name to be called out loud. I wanted people to cheer for me. I wanted an audience. Not because I didn't get approval at home. No, that was just who I was.

By the time I entered high school I had switched to defense and was getting more recognition for my on-field achievements. But I had finally learned to play for fun, not for recognition, and I had no desire to play in college. Then all of a sudden God opened a door.

A friend's dad was on the board of regents for Vanderbilt University. Though Vanderbilt had solid academics, their football program was struggling. When it came to athletic prowess, my friend was on the lower end of the spectrum, but he was going to a football camp to show off his skills. His dad invited me to come along, so I went.

My friend and I showed up and did all the drills, ran routes, and generally showed the coaches what we could do. At the end of the camp, they met with some of the attendees and gave their feedback. They assessed me as an okay player with raw talent. At first I was encouraged by what sounded like good news to me, but I soon found out that "raw talent" in football terms means they don't think you're very good. So I returned home and didn't think too much about the possibility of playing college football—that is, until I went to another football camp a few weeks later.

My brother had heard about a football camp at the University of Southern California, whose football team was a perennial powerhouse. They had just won two consecutive national championships and were going for a third. My family had friends in California, so we figured we would go to the camp and make a family trip out of it. There was only one problem: this was an invitation-only camp, and my brother and I weren't invited. Unfortunately, we didn't know this until after we had flown there from Texas with the expectation that we could participate. Talk about awkward. There was no restroom stall for me to hide in either. (Literally. We couldn't even get inside the locker room!) But by the grace of God, they let us in. They looked at their list, and even though we weren't on it, they allowed us to join the other kids on the field. This invitation came to mean everything.

We were at USC's Top 300 camp, which meant they invited the three hundred best high school football players in the state of California to see if they had what it would take to play football in college. I was there only because my brother wanted to go. Halfway through the camp, while going through some drills, I was told to go to a different station and repeat one of the drills. I was confused because

I thought I had done pretty well in that specific drill and didn't understand why they were singling me out. But I obliged.

These were one-on-one drills. You were pitted against an opponent to see who would win. I was playing defensive end at the time and was going against an offensive lineman, the position I used to play and hated. I had a field day. I loved competing and was having fun, so beating the other players was easy. I continued with the rest of the camp, thinking nothing of it. But then something happened.

Four other players and I were called up to the head coach's office. Five players out of three hundred. I didn't realize that the reason they called me back to do the drill a second time was because the assistant coaches saw I was doing well and wanted Pete Carroll, the head coach, to take a look. He liked what he saw and called me up. Sometimes God holds us back for our benefit.

"Sam," he said, "we were extremely impressed with what you did out there. You are a talented player, and we are interested in possibly offering you a scholarship."

I was floored. Vanderbilt had just told me they saw I had raw talent but weren't interested. USC, the best school in football at the time, was prepared to offer me a full ride.

He continued, "I'm going to talk with some of the coaches and get in touch with you in the next few weeks about coming to play football here at USC."

I was stunned. I couldn't believe USC was interested in me. But as I was enjoying the moment, I remembered something.

"Coach," I said. "In about two weeks I'll be going to

Nigeria with my family for medical mission work. Service is horrible out there, and I don't know if my phone will work. So if you call and I don't pick up, it's not because I don't like you but because I'm out of town."

"Not a problem," he said. "We'll be in touch."

With that I shook his hand and walked away. Two weeks later, while at the airport and preparing to board the plane, my phone rang. It was Ken Norton Jr., the recruiting coordinator for the school. He offered me a scholarship. But to everyone's surprise—most of all mine—I had to say no.

USC had been my dream school. The weather, the team, even the business school. But something was off.

In our conversation after the camp, they suggested I add about fifty pounds and play defensive tackle. I was already a big kid, and quite honestly, I was self-conscious about my size. So the prospect of adding another fifty pounds did not excite me. Plus, my dad knew some guys who had played professional sports, and they were now having serious medical issues. They had either gained too much weight and were having heart issues because of it or they had suffered too many injuries. The coaches assured me that if I made the switch, I would be a first-round pick one day in the NFL. Still, I wasn't comfortable.

Being a first-round pick wasn't the most important thing to me. And I knew that people sometimes lie to get what they want. Something just didn't feel right to me.

"Well," Coach Norton said, "I have Pete Carroll right next to me, and he's ready for you to commit. All you have to do is tell him you want to be a Trojan, and the deal is done."

Six simple words and the deal would be done: *I want to*

*be a Trojan.* But short and simple phrases often have long and heavy implications. And something wasn't sitting well in my spirit. What I didn't yet know was that, even as a teenager, the spirit of God was already guiding me.

After a few minutes of small talk, Coach Carroll asked, "Is there anything you would like to say before we get off the phone?"

Six words and my life would be forever changed.

"Coach," I said. "I would love the opportunity to one day . . . consider . . . the potential . . . of being something like a Trojan."

"Huh?" he replied, puzzled by my evasiveness.

"Coach, I've got to go. The plane is taking off. Talk later, bye."

With that I hung up.

My dad looked at me as if I were crazy. His entire expression screamed, *What have you done?* I didn't know. But something inside me couldn't say yes.

The next fourteen hours were the longest of my life. I questioned my decision and wondered why I couldn't just say yes. But when we landed in Nigeria, everything changed. There was something about that place, those people, that changed my perspective. I had been worried about whether I had made the right choice, but these people didn't know where their next meal was coming from. Yet they were fine. Perspective changes everything. I've heard it said that the less you have, the less you have to worry about. The people here weren't worried. They trusted God. He had provided for them before, and they were certain he would provide for them again.

I continued to serve, grow, and learn from the people there. People who couldn't care less about status and the number of followers someone has on social media. People who couldn't care less about other people's opinions of them. People there couldn't care less about their image. Their sole focus was on their God. He was their provider, their protector, their present help. He was their promise that their tomorrow would be better than their today.

That trip helped to shape me. People in Nigeria showed me that I would be okay as long as I trusted in God. And I did.

As soon as I returned to the States my phone started buzzing. When I looked at it, I saw I had over fifty missed calls and more than thirty-seven voice mails from college coaches all across the country. Two things had happened while I was away. My high school computer science teacher had put a video of some of my playing highlights on the recruiting website Rivals. And other teams had heard about the USC offer.

I received scholarship offers from schools all around the country. I decided to go to the University of Texas at Austin. God had shown up. I had put my trust in him. I was me. And I didn't try to be what everyone else thought I should be. God honored that.

We serve a God who created us for a purpose. He gave us unique experiences, personalities, and life stories for a reason; namely, to show us his love and to invite us to get to know him better. Know Jesus. Know peace. I found peace during my stay in Nigeria. And I found me. I was doing the things I loved and loving the people around me. I got to know Jesus there. I saw him in the hope that others had. I saw him in their smiles. I saw him in their peace. I got to know him intimately.

Even after I made it to the University of Texas, I had some believing to do. Though I was at one of the best schools in the nation, I still felt like I wasn't enough. There were times at practice when I thought I would never be able to measure up. There were times after practice when I strongly considered quitting. But God brought someone into my life to remind me of who he had made me to be.

> I saw [Jesus] in the hope that others had. I saw him in their smiles. I saw him in their peace.

Arthur Webb was my dad's friend. He also happened to be a team doctor for the Washington Redskins. During the summer before my senior year in college, he and I had a conversation that changed my life forever.

"Sam," he said, "I don't think you realize how good you can be."

He caught me off guard. Partly because I was eating and in mid-bite, but also because he and I hadn't had many conversations before. And definitely not about football.

"What do you mean?" I asked.

"I work with professional football players for a living. I see them every week after their games. You are just as big, fast, strong, and smart as all of them. But you're only missing one thing."

I waited.

"The only difference between you and all those other guys I see on a weekly basis is this: belief." He explained,

"Each and every one of those guys knew beyond a shadow of a doubt, far before they ever made it to the NFL, that they were going to make it. There was never a doubt in their minds. And that belief is what you're missing."

He described certain well-known players. He talked about how their actions, their work habits, and their eating habits changed. All based on this belief.

At that moment, I began to believe. And everything changed. I began to see God's glory in my life and in my play.

Dr. Webb helped me to see who I was as a football player. And those kids in that Nigerian village reminded me of who I was, but not as a football player. They reminded me that there is more to life than football, that there is more to life than anything this world can offer. And that is this: the opportunity, the invitation, the open door to get to know Jesus intimately. Once you know him, everything will change. I guarantee it.

## chapter fifteen

# DRAFT DAY

Statistics indicate a high school football player has a 0.2 percent chance of making it to the NFL. For the longest time, I didn't believe I was in that 0.2 percent. But after spending time with Arthur Webb and making the most of the opportunity to play in college, I believed my odds were improving. Still, I wasn't sure.

I met with different scouts whose job was to evaluate talent, and they had given me a draft grade as a possible midround selection. That was exciting news because the NFL draft was seven rounds long, and third, fourth, or fifth sounded good to me. How awesome would that be? But then I heard even more exciting news. I was told that if I excelled in the college all-star game, the NFL Scouting Combine, and my interviews with the teams, my draft stock would rise.

But first I had to have an agent.

The agent selection process is interesting. There were

several agents who wanted to represent me, and it was up to me to choose the right one. I was only twenty-one years old, though, and this was a big decision. Not only because they would negotiate my contract but also because they would be integral in deciding where I was going to prepare for the three big events leading up to the draft.

I was to meet with an agent and discuss where I would train for these big events. Each agent had agreements with certain facilities, where the agent would pay for the training and the facility would pay the agent to bring in the best players. But I already knew exactly where I wanted to train: Athletes' Performance Institute (API). This place was well known among college players. It was *the* place to go if you wanted to be a high draft pick. I was determined to get there and wasn't going to let an agent stop me. Thankfully, God had very different plans.

During a dinner with a potential agent, he tried to sell me on the idea of going to a different, smaller facility called Ignition Athletics Performance Group. *You're not going to fool me*, I thought. *Just because you're not affiliated with the top program doesn't mean I won't be.* But then he showed me a brochure that had a picture of a group of men holding hands and praying. They were all wearing shirts that said in big, bold letters: "Proverbs 27:17: As iron sharpens iron, so one person sharpens another." I was floored. Rarely do you see such an open display of faith in this profession. I had to find out more.

When I read the brochure, not only did I see open displays of faith, but I also saw great results. At that point, my mind was made up. After meeting with the agent, I called the facility. A man by the name of Clif Marshall picked up.

Clif was the performance director of this faith-based facility that focused on developing men in three ways: mind, body, and spirit. Clif was himself. He was unashamed of his faith in Christ and unashamed to be the best at his profession. We talked for more than an hour, and at that point, without an agent, I decided I would train at Ignition for the NFL Combine.

My time there was great. We trained physically, grew spiritually, and served in our community. Numbers were important, but they weren't the only thing. Clif knew our lives had much greater meaning than in what round we got drafted. So we trained, we prayed, we served, and God received the glory. But it wasn't without its share of disappointment.

I trained harder than I ever had in my life. I changed my diet, adjusted my sleep schedule, and pushed myself to the limit. All to increase my draft stock and reach my goal. It seemed to be paying off. I remembered what the scouts said about increasing my draft stock: Senior Bowl, the combine, and interviews. So I went to work.

The first step was the Senior Bowl. It is an all-star game that NFL prospects go through to show the coaches they can compete. You practice, train, and play in front of coaches from all thirty-two teams. God showed up for me there. I won most outstanding performance in the game and played well against top talent. First mission complete.

The next step was the NFL Combine. The combine is the event every coach, player, and scout talks about when it comes time for the draft. It is where you meet many NFL executives face-to-face for the first time. It is also where you run the coveted forty-yard dash. The forty, along with the three-cone drill and the short shuttle, are all drills the teams use to see where they will draft a player. If you perform well enough, your draft stock could easily rise. The only problem for me was that I had been struggling in the weeks leading up to the combine.

I practiced hard every day, but I couldn't seem to get my footwork down for the drills, the three-cone drill in particular. *One, two, touch. One, two, touch. One, two, three, four, five, finish.* And now, only two days from the combine, my training was over. I had just completed a mock combine at the Ignition facility, and Clif saw that I was frustrated and stressed. He has a heart for people and a heart for God. He knew something was up. Then he gave me a piece of advice that changed everything.

"Sam," he said, "you are doing great. But you and I both know you can't do it alone. So before you go to the combine and do those drills in front of all those coaches, I want you to pray this simple prayer: Joshua 1:9. Pray that God would give you the strength and courage to run your fastest times ever."

I was confused. I knew you needed strength to run fast, but the courage part threw me. Then I remembered the passage he mentioned.

God was speaking to Joshua, who had just taken over for Moses and was getting ready to lead God's people into the promised land. He must have been scared because God had to remind him three times to be strong and courageous. Finally, God said to him, "Have I not commanded you? Be strong and courageous. Do not be afraid; do not be discouraged, for the LORD your God will be with you wherever you go" (Josh. 1:9).

It's so easy to get discouraged sometimes. To think you're not good enough. To stop believing and start doubting. Sometimes we need to be reminded, not of who we are but who we're with: "The LORD your God will be with you *wherever* you go." Even at the NFL Combine.

I showed up, got in my stance, and I prayed. One of the little-known rules in the forty-yard dash is that after you get into your stance, you have to be still for two seconds before you can run. If you move, you're disqualified. It's interesting how hard it is to be still. I think we should apply this principle to all of life's situations: be still—even if it's just for two seconds—and pray. You'd be surprised by the amount of peace you receive. Thank God for the situation, good or bad. Ask God for wisdom. Ask him for confidence. Ask him for courage. Paul said that God did not give us a spirit of fear but of power, love, and a sound mind (2 Timothy 1:7). Pray. Always. And watch as God shows up.

In that moment, I prayed, God, *give me the strength and courage to run my fastest time ever.*

And he did.

I was a top performer in the forty-yard dash and the short shuttle. I also set an all-time record in the three-cone drill, the drill I feared the most. I'll never forget the looks on the scouts' faces when they saw my time. It was a look of utter shock and disbelief. But I knew what had happened. God had shown up. Second mission complete.

The last hurdle was the interviews with the coaches. Some of my interviews took place at the combine, but most took place at my university. Coaches from different teams visited the campus and met with me one on one.

These meetings could be intimidating. They would begin in the meeting room. The coach would draw up a play on the whiteboard and explain the assignments and responsibilities of all eleven guys on defense and see if you had any questions. After that he would erase the board and start some small talk. He would ask about your family, your upbringing, your love for the game, and any off-field issues you may have had during your high school and college years. He would then review some videos of your best and worst games. If there was a play in which you weren't giving your full effort or in which you made a glaring mistake, he'd ask about it. Your good and bad performances were all called into question. He'd ask what defense your team was running and what your responsibility was on a particular play. He'd ask about your favorite calls and the calls you most hated. He'd ask about your relationship with your coaches and teammates. No topic was off-limits.

Once the interview concluded, he would shake your hand and thank you for meeting with him. At this point you would think the meeting was over and stand to leave, but before you went, he would ask, "Do you remember that play I showed you at the beginning of the meeting? Can you draw it up for me?" Then you would have to draw up as much of the play as you remembered. This included the name of the play and the assignments, alignments, and techniques of all eleven defensive players. You also would have to include an offensive formation and route combination.

Needless to say, it is an intense process. But by the grace

of God and through rigorous preparation, I succeeded. I wasn't perfect, but I don't think I was expected to be. The coaches wanted to see how I reacted. They wanted to see if I was poised under pressure. They wanted to see if I would crack. They wanted to see me. And they did. They saw me. They saw my good, my bad, even my ugly. And I was enough.

You, too, are enough. Your best plays and your worst plays are a part of your story. There's no need to hide. Let the world see you. Third mission complete.

Everything had gone according to plan. My agent was speaking with several teams, and he told me my draft stock was on the rise. I had gone from a third-, fourth-, or fifth-round selection to a second- or third-round prospect, with a possibility of going in the first. I was excited. But that excitement turned into doubt and disappointment much sooner than I thought possible.

The first round of the 2011 NFL draft took place on a Thursday. I knew my chances weren't great in the first round, but I threw a draft party anyway, inviting friends and family to experience *my* big moment with me. God has a funny way of humbling people. The first round came and went, and I wasn't drafted. I wasn't worried though. Second and third rounds were still to come.

> You, too, are enough. Your best plays and your worst plays are a part of your story. There's no need to hide. Let the world see you.

The next two rounds of the draft took place on Friday. I was certain this was going to be my day. My agent had promised me as much. My coaches had promised me as much. Everyone had promised me but God.

During the weeks leading up to the draft I had visits with and phone calls from several teams. One team brought me in for a visit, and after the meeting, the coach assured me I would be their second-round pick, third at the latest. During a meeting with another team, the head coach said he was eager to see me in their uniform. I called my agent, and he relayed what he was hearing from many other teams.

"Sam, you've done an outstanding job thus far. It really couldn't have gone any better. All the feedback I've got from the teams is that you have moved up on their draft board. Twenty-seven of the thirty-two teams have you projected in the second or third round."

He was sure. I was sure. There was no doubt. But there was a little bit of pride. I thought *I* had done it. *I* had achieved my goals. And now it was time for the teams to follow through on their end of the bargain.

They didn't.

The second and third rounds came and went, and my phone didn't ring. I felt tricked. The coaches who said they would draft me in the second round had deceived me. My agent who said I would go in the third round at the latest had failed me. Plus, all those people I invited to my draft party were looking at me, unsure of what to say. I didn't know what to say either, but all eyes were on me, so I finally said, "Thank you all for coming. I obviously didn't plan this, but God is good." But I didn't believe it.

I told everyone goodbye and didn't schedule a draft party for the next day, which was for the fourth through seventh rounds and for the guys who would be invited to training camps as undrafted free agents. I was so sure I was better than the guys in those rounds. Proverbs 18:12 says, "Before a downfall the heart is haughty, but humility comes before honor." And I had been humbled.

I went to my room that night and cried uncontrollable tears. My tears didn't stem from not being drafted in the first three rounds; they stemmed from the lies I had been told. I didn't know who to believe anymore. I also didn't know if I was even going to have an opportunity to play in the NFL. My confidence was depleted. Then I got on my knees and cried out to God:

> *God, you know my heart. I'm doing this for you. Not for anyone else. You see me. You know me. You know I don't care about the money or the fame. I just want to give you glory. Please, God, give me this opportunity. I don't care if I even get drafted. Just give me a chance, and I will bring your name glory. Amen.*

After that I slept. I woke up the next morning unsure of what time the draft started, but I wasn't going to wait around all day. My confidence in the coaches was gone. My confidence now was in God alone. I went downstairs and we ordered breakfast. My sister picked up the food, and my family and I blessed the meal. As soon as we said amen, the phone rang. It was the Arizona Cardinals. They called to tell me they were going to draft me. I didn't believe them. I turned on the television and was determined to stay on the phone with them until I saw it with my own eyes.

"Sam," the team owner said, "we need to hang up so we can call the league office and tell them we're drafting you."

I reluctantly agreed.

Funny enough, the draft cut to a commercial as my name was being called. I think God wanted to remind me that it still wasn't about me. It was about him.

God knows us well. He gives us exactly what we need when we need it. He doesn't make mistakes. We just have to wait for him. We have to cry out to him. And he will answer us. It may not be the answer we expect, but it's always the answer we need.

Be strong and courageous. Be still. Cry out to God. He will hear your prayer.

## chapter sixteen

# THE FINAL CHAPTER

I would be remiss if I didn't tell you how this book came about. After a tumultuous 2018, a year in which I lost nearly everything, I gained so much more than I ever imagined.

Soon after Jerry died, Ngozi's wallet was stolen from a gym. A stolen wallet is bad enough, but what made it even more difficult for us was that my wife is not a US citizen; she is a temporary resident. And her temporary residence card was in her wallet.

We had planned a trip to South Korea for our five-year wedding anniversary. One of my friends from Thunderbird was an administrator at George Mason University's South Korea campus and had been inviting me to speak there for years. I figured this year I would carve out some time for the trip. Well, the way it turned out, I didn't have to carve out any time for the trip. God had carved it out for me.

Have you ever been so busy you felt like you didn't have time to catch your breath? Well, God doesn't like that. He wants us to slow down and enjoy his presence. Enjoy his creation. Someone said that if Satan can't make you bad, he'll make you busy. And I had been busy. Busyness seems good at first.

**If Satan can't make you bad, he'll make you busy.**

We get a lot accomplished. We build up our résumés. We earn the approval of people. We're being productive. But sometimes I wonder if God is pleased with our busyness.

I'm reminded of two psalms:

> One thing have I asked of the LORD,
> that will I seek after:
> that I may dwell in the house of the LORD
> all the days of my life,
> to gaze upon the beauty of the LORD
> and to inquire in his temple. (Ps. 27:4 ESV)

> Be still before the LORD and wait patiently for
> him. (Ps. 37:7 ESV)

Our society places a premium on accomplishments over abiding, on doing over dwelling. But God's standards haven't changed since the days of the Psalter. His desires haven't either.

My dad recently reminded me of this truth. He pointed me to Scripture and reminded me that we need to change our focus. I realized *I* needed to change my focus. I was so busy being busy. But it wasn't how I was meant to live. It wasn't how any of us are meant to live. We aren't meant to rush through life and worry about the future. We are created to abide, to dwell, to inquire.

This reminds me of my kids. All my kids want to do is to be close to me. That's it. They want to play, to run around, to abide. It's so beautiful. And it's a picture of what God desires from us. He wants us to be close to him. He wants us to meditate and marinate in his presence, in his Word, in Scripture. He wants us to know him really, really well. That's all he desires. Back then, when my kids wanted to be close to me, I was always too busy. So God had to slow me down.

After my friend passed and Ngozi's wallet was stolen, our house flooded. It was the weekend of the polar vortex, where temperatures in Chicago dropped to as low as −50 degrees Fahrenheit. That week Chicago was literally the coldest place on earth. Colder than Antarctica, Alaska, Russia, and the North Pole. Thankfully my family and I were out of town. But my house wasn't. A pipe burst and everything flooded. We were in Atlanta for the Super Bowl when I got a phone call from a frantic neighbor.

"I hope you're okay, Sam," he began.

Constantine had moved to Chicago from Russia not too long ago, so he knew about cold weather. He called me after his daughter got home from school and saw our house leaking. From my end of the phone call, it sounded as if it were raining where he was. It wasn't. My front door was soaked, and water was leaking from the top down. It wasn't pretty. God was faithful though.

We came back from Atlanta and packed up our stuff. Not too much was damaged, but our place was unlivable. Plus the floors were soaked, the power had been turned off, and it was freezing. We needed a place to stay.

Thankfully I have good teammates. As soon as Trey Burton heard the news, he called and offered his home for us to stay in.

Soon after, we began looking for a place to move but found nothing that would work. Ngozi and I searched diligently. We were happy about Trey's hospitality, but we hoped to get settled elsewhere. I still had another year on my contract with the Bears, and we had a five-month-old baby. We had been looking for something bigger before the flood, but now we were fully motivated in our search. Yet days passed, three weeks went by, and we found nothing. Then, when we finally found a place we liked and were ready to move in, the owner took it off the market just days before we could close. Finding a house in Chicago wasn't working out for us, and I soon found out why.

Exactly three weeks after the flood, my phone rang. The head coach and the general manager informed me I was going to be released from the team.

I had never been released before, never been fired, and frankly, I didn't know how to respond. I thanked them for the opportunity to play for the team and got off the phone. With everything going on—the theft, the injury, the benching, the flood, the car accident, the loss of Jerry, and now my release—things felt a little crazy.

The image in my mind as I hung up was of a blizzard. It

was as if I were inside a snow globe, standing glued to the ground while it was being shaken all around. But, at the same time, it didn't feel like everything was out of control. It was as if God was holding the snow globe, and he was doing the shaking. Though there was movement in all directions, I didn't feel out of place. I felt I was right in the palm of God's hand. I was reminded of Psalm 37:23–24:

> The LORD makes firm the steps
> of the one who delights in him;
> though he may stumble, he will not fall,
> for the LORD upholds him with his hand.

The other image I had was that of the main character in a story about my life. A chapter had ended, but I didn't have the power to turn the page. I had to wait for God to do it. No matter what you're going through in life, know that God is writing your story. Don't skip ahead. Don't rush the process. Don't lose hope. The story isn't done yet.

❧

God is faithful. Since our house had flooded, we already had all our stuff packed and put into storage before I was released. God is kind that way. He is compassionate. He has ways of managing our pain and giving it to us in doses we can handle. He knows our frame.

Now we were without a house, without a car, without a job, without a mentor, and without a passport. And the trip to South Korea that we had been planning for months was just a few days away. So I either needed to cancel the trip or spend my five-year anniversary alone and overseas. I asked Ngozi what she thought. She told me to go.

Up until that point I still hadn't slowed down. Not just in that year but for the last several years. I was moving at a hectic pace and barely took time to breathe. God finally had to stop me. He had to slow me down and get me alone. Why? Because he knew I needed it. I needed to hear his voice.

&

"What do you do for a living?" the flight attendant asked politely. She saw I had been writing notes for hours. We had minor interactions during the fourteen-hour flight, and the plane was now getting ready to land.

"I'm a football player," I responded. "Headed to give a talk and host a football camp at a school in South Korea."

"You don't look like a football player," she said.

I stopped, slightly offended, and wondered if I needed to get back in the weight room so I could fill out my shirt some more. But that's not what she meant.

"Football players are supposed to be mean," she said. "And you're so . . . nice."

She had called something out in me that I had yet to come to terms with myself: I was more than what people saw on the football field. I was more than what people expected me to be.

That trip proved to be life changing. After speaking

at the school and hosting a football clinic in the gym, I was left alone in a hotel room. Seven thousand miles away from family and friends. My host had set aside time for Ngozi and me to spend together while we were there, but since Ngozi couldn't come, I was by myself. So I decided to rest.

But all of a sudden God woke me up. He woke me up, and I started writing. And writing. And writing. Words just began to flow. It was as if a section of my heart that had been marked off-limits for years had finally been opened. Being still will do that to you. I tried to sleep but couldn't. I just wrote. I wrote about life. I wrote about death. I wrote about fear. I wrote about shame. I just wrote. And I haven't stopped writing.

A few months before the trip, after sharing with a friend some of what was going on in my life, he said something interesting. In the midst of my pain, doubt, struggles, and fear, he offered an opinion: "It just may be that God is writing a book in your life. And who knows, you may be only on chapter 2."

He was right. In the time that followed, subsequent chapters came to life. And thus, this book began.

Starting a book is one thing. Finishing it is completely different.

I started writing this book not long after I had been released. I had fired my agent months before. We've had our fair share of disagreements and blowups, and I figured it was time to move on. The breakup didn't go well. No one likes to be fired, and I was being a little immature. We hadn't talked in months, and I had no intention of reaching out to him. But God was starting to change my heart. He was teaching me about forgiveness. He was teaching me about reconciliation. He was teaching me about love.

Months passed, and I couldn't shake this feeling that something wasn't right. My agent and I hadn't ended on good terms, and though I didn't want to admit it, I may have been the one at fault. I couldn't shake this feeling that I needed to call him and apologize. Sometimes God nudges us in this way. In fact, Jesus did more than nudge. He straight up told it like it is: "For if you forgive others their trespasses, your heavenly Father will also forgive you, but if you do not forgive others their trespasses, neither will your Father forgive your trespasses" (Matt. 6:14–15 ESV).

So, after arguing with God for a bit, I picked up the phone and dialed my agent's number. I had no idea what to expect. I knew he was still upset, but I didn't know how he would respond. I also hadn't signed with a team and needed some advice on what to do next. I may have needed new representation as well. But more important, I needed to fix a broken relationship.

Forgiving someone who hurt you is hard. You may still feel some of the pain you felt when you were hurt. But God forgave you, and because of that, you should forgive others. This truth is what Jesus reminded the people of in Matthew 6. He was healing people of their diseases, sicknesses, and pain. He was also teaching in the synagogues, letting people know the good news about the kingdom of heaven. But he was mourning. Mourning for the people and their condition, both physical and spiritual. He had seen the abysmal state of mankind. They were distant from God. So Jesus came and gave them some clarity on what God desires for his children. God forgave us for our sins against him, even while we were in the middle of doing them. He forgave us, and Jesus called us to do the same for each other. I had to make the call.

My agent had been deeply hurt by the way things went down. I had been too. I apologized to him for the way I handled the situation. He forgave me. We cried, we reconciled, and we formed a deeper bond.

"You know what," he said. "I've never had as much respect for you as a person as I do now. Don't get me wrong. I've had respect for you as a football player. But as a person, to be frank, I've had my ups and downs. But this Sam is different, and I like him."

Real men apologize. Real women do too. It's time to forgive.

This singular decision, the decision to forgive, would be one of the most life-altering decisions of my life. I learned that by being me I can be loved, respected, and accepted. Regardless of my profession, regardless of my title. You can too.

Our friendship grew. As did our love for each other. And though he wasn't officially representing me, he unofficially played a huge role in my next career move.

In the months after the Bears released me, I still hadn't signed with another team. This was the longest I had ever been a free agent. But something was changing within me. My desires were shifting. It seemed as if God was giving me some time. Time to breathe, time to be a dad, time to find new desires. He was preparing me for a transition. And though I did get anxious at times, a good friend reminded me that this free time was a luxury, an added benefit.

"Money," she said, "can be replicated. You lose it, you gain it. The only thing in this life that can't be replicated is our time. God is giving you this time off as a gift. Take advantage of it."

This time off would, in fact, prove beneficial. I was being me, taking life one day at a time, and allowing God to order my steps, just as his Word says: "Trust in the LORD with all your heart, and do not lean on your own understanding. In all your ways acknowledge him, and he will make straight your paths" (Prov. 3:5–6 ESV).

At the time, it didn't make sense why I wasn't playing, but I felt at peace. I bought a house, spent time with my wife and kids, and sought God's face. As I was listening, the spirit of God assured me that I would have another opportunity to play football, but it would only come after I completed my book. I went back to work on it and continued writing for month after month. Finally, with one chapter left—this chapter—and minutes after signing my agreement with the publisher and sending over my official contract, my phone rang.

It was my former agent. The guy I had become friends with months prior. A team had a need, and for some reason they still had his phone number listed as my contact.

He called me with the good news, and then he did the unexpected: he volunteered to unofficially help me in whatever way I needed. He advised me on the best negotiation tactics, called the contact person, and put me in touch with the right people on the team. All free of charge, and free of pretenses. He was my friend, and it was special. I told him about this final chapter and how I had been thinking of him the last few days. He was honored. As was I.

I worked out for the team, but for reasons that were not clear to me, they did not sign me. I was confused. And to be honest, I was ready to be done with playing football.

Initially I thought the transition would be easy. After all, I felt like I had done a good job of not putting my identity in my career, but I was wrong. Identity issues, even if you are careful, can sneak up on you in a heartbeat.

Every Sunday and most Mondays during that season, I was either stressed out, angry, or in tears. The tears would usually come Sunday morning when I was at church, sometime during worship. I'm not sure if it was the songs they were playing or the fact that I was in a church on Sunday morning instead of at a stadium, but I was mourning. Games were being played, and I wasn't a part of them. Sunday after Sunday after Sunday it hit me like a ton of bricks. And if I wasn't crying, I was feeling irritated with those around me. Especially Ngozi and the kids. Mondays were no better. Monday Night Football was constantly hanging over

> Identity issues, even if you are careful, can sneak up on you in a heartbeat.

my head, reminding me of the opportunities I was missing. Sundays and Mondays were hard.

"Maybe you should consider not watching the games," my dad suggested. That advice helped, but there were still days when I felt "less than." It felt like a notch from my imaginary belt of achievement had been removed. I wondered what people would know me for now. How they would see me. But slowly, and ever so lovingly, God reminded me of who I was. A father. A friend. A writer.

Much of this book was written during this time. God was showing me parts of myself that I had ignored for years. He was allowing me to see myself before showing me off to the world. God was doing a new work in me.

This book was born out of adversity. Born out of pain. Born out of doubt, fear, and anxiety. But that's not all that made this book. This book was also born out of freedom. A freedom of believing that you and I are both worth getting to know. A freedom of believing that we have a God in heaven who knows us *and* loves us deeply. This book was born out of faith. Faith that God was writing a bigger story in my life. He's writing one in yours too. The pain was a part of his plan. It always is.

I didn't know how to write this final chapter. I wasn't sure how the story was going to end. And in many ways, I still don't know. But what I have come to realize is that God knows. He knew all along. He is teaching me who I am and showing me that I am worth getting to know. The real me.

In some ways, on some days, I'm starting to understand that. Like the day I left to work out with the team I was sure would sign me. I kissed Ngozi goodbye and loaded my bags in the vehicle that would take me to the airport.

"Are you a soldier?" the driver asked.

"No," I responded. "I'm a football player. . . . I'm a writer too."

[God] is teaching me who I am and showing me that I am worth getting to know. The real me.

You are more than the sum of your past mistakes. You are loved. You are known. *You are worth getting to know.*

# CONCLUSION

## *Love*

I started this book by telling you how I lost my friend Jerry. He told me two things. The first is what this book is all about: *you are worth getting to know.* I spent the better part of this book and the last few years learning that truth for myself and allowing people to see me. This revelation has helped me grow tremendously. But this truth isn't the most important part of what Jerry left with me, though. The most important part was this: get to know Jesus.

God is love. And love never ends. God loves us so much that he sacrificed his own son, Jesus, so we could be close to him. So he could make his home within us. So his peace could reign in our minds and in our hearts forever. There's an intimacy that God deeply desires with us, his greatest creation. He wants us to seek after him in the good times and the bad times. He wants us to know him, know his love, and know his son. Get to know Jesus.

When you get to know Jesus, you get to experience love.

And not just any kind of love, but a *never-ending love*. A love that lasts a lifetime and then some. What I gather from Galatians 4:9 is that to know God is to be known by God. It's similar to what Paul wrote in 1 Corinthians 13:12: "Now I know in part; then I shall know fully, even as I have been fully known" (ESV).

It seems to me that to get to fully know God, we need to allow ourselves to be fully known by God. And because I am confident God already fully knows us, to get to know God is to come to the understanding that God already knows us, even when we hide. That truth is what I experienced at every turn, in every chapter. He is a God who already knows. He knows your quirks, your disabilities, your inefficiencies. He made them! And he is sufficient even when you're not. And if you don't believe me, consider Psalm 139. God formed our parts and put us together in the womb. We have all been fearfully and wonderfully made. And he has mapped out every day of our lives (vv. 13–14). Finally, the psalm ends with:

> To know God is to be known by God.

> Search me, O God, and know my heart!
>> Try me and know my thoughts!
> And see if there be any grievous way in me,
>> and lead me in the way everlasting! (vv. 23–24 ESV)

It seems to me that we were known well before we even realized it. And this truth brings me joy.

There's a story in the gospel of John about a man with

glaring insufficiencies: he was a blind beggar. The man was shunned by many people because of his blindness. And this included even the disciples of Jesus, the people closest to him. They wouldn't allow the man to come anywhere near Jesus. (Thankfully the people *closest* to Jesus aren't Jesus.) They asked him what caused the man's blindness. Was it his sin? Was it his parents' sin? Who made the mistake? Jesus' response is startlingly beautiful: "It was not that this man sinned, or his parents, but that the works of God might be displayed in him" (9:3 ESV).

What works is God trying to display in your life through your story? Through your weaknesses? Through your strengths? What lies have you been believing about your life's circumstances?

Moments later, Jesus healed this man who had been born blind. But Jesus said something interesting in the interim: "As long as I am in the world, I am the light of the world" (v. 5 ESV).

Jesus then spat in some dirt, rubbed the mud on the man's eyes, and told him to wash it off in a nearby pool. When the man did as he was told, he was healed. After being healed, the man told everyone about what God had done for him.

We should have this type of joy. Both after and *before* God helps us with our situation. Allow God to light up your past and brighten your future. God is love. Love is patient. Love is kind. Love never ends.

Get to know Jesus. Better yet, allow Jesus to get to know you. Your deficiencies, your faults, your fears, your failures. And then share them with the world.

~

Sometimes it can be difficult to find out who you are, especially when you've been living in fear for a better part of your life. But here are a few suggestions for how you can be real in a world full of fakes.

**1. Pray.** Psalm 37:4 says, "Delight yourself in the LORD, and he will give you the desires of your heart" (ESV). One of my prayers recently has been that God would show me my desires. Ask God to show you yours. Pray that God would show you more about who you are and more about who he is. He desperately wants to be known. He wants to be sought after. In James 4:8 we're reminded, "Draw near to God, and he will draw near to you" (ESV). Give it a shot. Even if you haven't tried before, now is always a great time to start.

**2. Try new things.** There are certain things you're passionate about or you may enjoy doing. Try them! I love talking, so I became a speaker. I also love kids, so I babysit from time to time. Don't be ashamed of your desires. God gave them to you for a reason! "For we are God's handiwork, created in Christ Jesus to do good works, which God prepared in advance for us to do" (Eph. 2:10). God already prepared the works for us to do. Now it's time to just do them. We're also reminded in Philippians 2:13 that God is already working in us: "For it is God who works in you, both to will and to work for his good pleasure" (ESV). Those ideas, those plans, those dreams that have been on your mind are there for a reason. Give them a shot.

**3. Read God's Word.** God tells us who we are in his Word. For those of you who feel unworthy or like a waste of space, read God's Word. He says in Ephesians 1 and 2 that you are blessed, you are chosen, you are holy, you are blameless, you are predestined, you are adopted, you are seated with Jesus in heavenly places, you are saved by grace, you are a fellow citizen, you are a member of the household of God. Moreover, you are being built into a dwelling place for God. He also says that you have been redeemed, forgiven, lavished upon, sealed with the Holy Spirit, made alive with Christ Jesus, saved by grace through faith, raised up with Christ Jesus, given a gift of God (salvation), brought near by the blood of Christ, made one with Christ Jesus, reconciled to God through the cross, and given access to the Father. You also have an inheritance in heaven. Read the rest of Ephesians. In it God tells you who you are.

**4. Listen to God in prayer.** Spend as much time as you can in prayer. "Never stop praying" (1 Thess. 5:17 ICB). Always keep a line of communication open with God. Prayer is a conversation, and a conversation involves both talking and listening. Spend as much time as you can in silence, listening for God's voice. It may seem odd at first, but the more you slow down and listen, the more affirmation and direction you will receive. Slow down and see where God directs you.

**5. Do not be afraid.** It's completely human to feel scared at times. But remember God's words: "Do not be afraid" (Josh. 1:9). I'm reminded of this truth all the time. Situations scare me, but God reminds me, just like he reminded Joshua, not to be afraid. Why? Because he is with us. "Even though I walk through the valley of the shadow of death, I will fear no evil, for you are with me; your rod and your staff, they comfort me" (Ps. 23:4 ESV). I get scared of people's opinions. I get scared of certain situations. I get scared of taking risks. But if I believe God is leading me to do something, I'll remind myself, *Do not be afraid*, then do it. And God always shows up.

Being you is not easy. You may be ridiculed, you may be put down, you may feel uncomfortable, you may not fit in at first. But God will be pleased. Be prepared for some bumps along the way. Be prepared for the growth that will come as well. Be prepared to be forever changed.

I'm at my best when I'm me. When I'm energetic, laughing, emoting, feeling, and loving. That's me. It has nothing to do with my job, nothing to do with my kids, nothing to do with my wife, nothing to do with my politics. It has everything to do with how God created me. Long before I had a job, I was me. Long before I had a wife, I was me. Long before I had kids, I was me. And even after having all those things, I'm still me.

God is in the business of constantly refining and growing us in order to teach us to be more like Jesus. Don't be surprised if some of your desires change. It's a part of the process.

Your biggest weaknesses can become your biggest strengths. When I was growing up, I was always a big kid. I hated it.

I was self-conscious about my weight, my size, my appearance. But God used that size for his good. He loves doing that. Using the areas you hide from the world and making them your point of greatest victory.

Moses didn't want to lead the people out of Egypt. He was scared and even argued with God, telling him all the reasons why he wasn't fit for the job. So God gave him Aaron to help him.

David was the youngest, smallest child of Jesse. He also was looked down upon because he was a shepherd. But David used his prowess as a shepherd to defeat Goliath.

Saul of Tarsus was a murderer. Yet Jesus met him and turned him around.

What is your area of weakness? Where does God want to use you?

For the longest time I put on a mask. I acted as if I was a macho, fearless, cutthroat jock. But in reality I was not that person. I'm loving, kind, and generous. Three words I never heard in my nine years of playing professional football. The way I see it, God made each of us unique for a reason. I used to watch sports as a kid and think I was not enough. Not big enough, not fast enough, not tough enough. But when I got older, I realized I am enough and that God made me this way for a reason. Actually, many reasons. I think one of the reasons God made me so caring is that he wanted to teach the world not to stereotype people.

People who play in the NFL, for better or for worse, are judged quickly. As are athletes in general. I think God wanted me to break down some barriers. To show people there's no such thing as being too nice to play in the NFL.

There's no such thing as too anything. You are the way you are because God made you that way. You don't need to fit in, you don't need to try to be like everyone else. You are different. And God loves that. But the only way you can learn about who you are is by learning as much as you can about the God who made you. Parents are great. Ancestors are fine too. But God planned it all out. He even planned that you would be exactly where you are right now, reading this book.

> You are the way you are because God made you that way. . . . You are different. And God loves that.

Be you. But first, get to know Jesus. Spend time with him. Read his Word. Pray. Listen. Allow the Word of God to transform you. But don't do it halfway. Give it your all. Rest in his presence. Allow God's love to saturate your soul. I promise, you won't regret it.

Jeremiah 29:12–13 promises, "Then you will call on me and come and pray to me, and I will listen to you. You will seek me and find me when you seek me with all your heart." God wants wholehearted believers. He doesn't do anything halfway. It's not in his nature.

# EPILOGUE

## *Learning to Listen*

There is an art to getting to know Jesus—namely, being still.

Long ago God created the heavens and the earth, the wind and the skies, animals and people. He created us in his image to be able to reason, create, live, and eventually spend eternity with him. He wanted relationship. He walked alongside us in the garden, and we enjoyed perfect relationship with him. But then God's creation made a choice, and we sinned. We decided that instead of enjoying the gifts of a good Creator, we wanted to *be* the good Creator. But that wasn't God's plan. He made us so we wouldn't have to experience the weight of good and evil. He just wanted us to be.

Sin altered our perfect relationship with God, but only for a little while. God always craved that relationship. It's in his nature. You see it so many times throughout the Bible. On ten separate occasions in Scripture, God reiterates this truth: I will be your God, you will be my people, and I will remember your sins no more. God wanted to remember our sins no more, to cast our sins as far as the east is from the west, to cleanse us of *all* unrighteousness. And last time I checked, *all* means *all*. You see this promise in Genesis 17:7–8, Exodus 6:7, Deuteronomy 29:13, Jeremiah 24:7 and 31:33, Hosea 2:23, Zechariah 8:8, 2 Corinthians 6:16, Hebrews 8:10–12, and Revelation 21:7. From the first book of the Bible to the last and everywhere in between, God constantly reminds us of his desire to know us and for us to know him: "The one who conquers will have this heritage, and I will be his God and he will be my son" (Rev. 21:7 ESV).

God invites us to have a relationship with him, to get to know him. Our God *loves* relationship. He loves us. So in order to rebuild his relationship with us, he sent his Son to make the ultimate sacrifice: to live the life we weren't able to live and die the death we weren't able to die.

For the longest time, Moses and the Israelites—and the generations after them—had to sacrifice a perfect animal to appease a perfect God and make things right. But these sacrifices were never intended to be forever. God sent his Son to show us what perfect sacrifice looks like. He lost so that we would win.

In the gospel of John, Jesus told his disciples:

The greatest love a person can show is to die for his friends. You are my friends if you do what I command you. I don't call you servants now. A servant does not know what his master is doing. But now I call you friends because I have made known to you everything I heard from my Father. You did not choose me; I chose you. And I gave you this work, to go and produce fruit. I want you to produce fruit that will last. Then the Father will give you anything you ask for in my name. This is my command: Love each other. (15:13–17 ICB)

In these verses, Jesus revealed just what God had been after all along: our friendship. And what do friends do? Friends spend time together. They recognize each other's voices. They know the kinds of things the other would say.

I have young kids. I spend a lot of time with them, as does Ngozi. As soon as she walks into the room and starts talking, their ears perk up, even if they haven't yet seen her. Ngozi could be in a different room, and they would know who it was without even seeing her because they know her voice from having spent so much time with her. God wants the same for us.

He wants us to spend so much time with him and so much time getting to know Jesus that we recognize his voice. It only takes a handful of scriptures to reveal the type of intimacy God desires to have with us:

> I will be their God,
>> and they shall be my people. . . .
>> and I will remember their sins no more.
>>> (Heb. 8:10, 12 ESV)

> Delight yourself in the LORD,
>> and he will give you the desires of your heart.
>>> (Ps. 37:4 ESV)

> Cast all your anxiety on him because he cares for you.
> (1 Peter 5:7)

If you get to know Jesus, you'll see how much he desires to get to know you too. It's not a one-way street. He knows what you're going through, and he is constantly offering you reminders of his love for you. But you won't know that unless you spend time getting to know him and listening to his voice. In the gospel of John, Jesus said:

> I am the good shepherd. I know my sheep, and my sheep know me, just as the Father knows me, and I know the Father. I give my life for the sheep. I have other sheep that are not in this flock here. I must bring them also. They will listen to my voice, and there will be one flock and one shepherd. The Father loves me because I give my life. I give my life so that I can take it back again. No one takes it away from me. I give my own life freely. I have the right to give my life, and I have the right to take it back. This is what my Father commanded me to do. (10:14–18 ICB)

This is love.

When God sent his Son, he sent him as a sacrifice. Jesus was sent so we could have access to God the Father. Jesus lived a perfect life, became a perfect sacrifice, died a horrific death, and then conquered death forever. But then he left. That part didn't make sense to me at first. Why would Jesus leave? He had died on the cross, had risen from the dead, and after all that, he was leaving? But thankfully, God's thoughts are higher than mine. Before Jesus left, he told his disciples: "If anyone loves me, he will keep my word, and my Father will love him, and we will come to him and make our home with him" (John 14:23 ESV). And earlier he told them, "I will ask the Father, and he will give you another Helper, to be with you forever" (v. 16 ESV).

All this time, God had been wanting to make his home with us. That's why he sent his Son. That's why he sent the Holy Spirit. With the Holy Spirit inside us, we can think like him and reason like him. God wants us to expand our vision. Jesus added:

> The Helper, the Holy Spirit, whom the Father will send in my name, he will teach you all things and bring to your remembrance all that I have said to you. Peace I leave with you; my peace I give to you. Not as the world gives do I give to you. Let not your hearts be troubled, neither let them be afraid. (vv. 26–27 ESV)

Access. No obstruction. No fear. That's what God is after. He wants to make his home with you. What an opportunity. What an honor.

Learn to listen to the words of Jesus. Become one of his sheep. Join the flock. If you do, you'll see the depth of his love for you.

> The Lord God gave me the ability to teach.
> He has taught me what to say to make the weak strong.

Every morning he wakes me.
He teaches me to listen like a student.
The Lord God helps me learn. (Isa. 50:4–5 ICB)

❧

I was dealing with a lot of doubt after the 2018 season. I was coming off an injury, and it seemed as if my desires were changing. Football no longer felt like a priority in my life, but I had just been signed to a new team, and I didn't want to let anyone down. I remember being in tears in a hotel room on the day of my first game with the new team. I was an emotional wreck and I had no idea why. I went to the game, played pretty well, but still felt like something was different. The weight of people's opinions began to matter less, and the sound of God's whisper became louder and louder.

At the last game of the preseason, on the day before the final cuts, I felt an immense sense of peace. Usually this was a time of year that was very stressful for me. There was a single game left to determine my future. But after getting to know Jesus a little bit better, I realized my future was already determined. God had good plans for me no matter the outcome. And he reminded me of this *during* the game.

Much like all those years ago when I was praying during the games for my swelling to cease, God's whisper became clearer and clearer: *I am so proud of you. So, so proud.* By this point I had begun to recognize the voice.

*Really?* I responded. *Even after that?*

Before I could complete another thought, I heard another whisper: *I'm so, so proud of you.*

The next day, for the second time in my NFL career, I was cut. My phone rang, and the staff member informed me of the news. Peace was all I felt. Peace. The weight was gone. The pressure was gone. I was one with my Savior. I knew him. I knew he had better things in store.

He did.

I spent the next two months being a dad to my kids, a husband to my wife, and a friend to my peers. Later that year I signed with the Tampa Bay Buccaneers and finished the season there. It's funny because I had just decided I was done playing football on Friday, and on Monday my phone rang. I wanted to say no, but as I prayed in that moment, all I could hear was: *say yes.* So I did.

I believe Jesus is asking you to say yes right now. Say yes to him. Say yes to peace. Say yes to letting the world see you. Say yes.

# ACKNOWLEDGMENTS

This book is a by-product of so many people that God put in my life. These words are just a small measure of my gratitude to you. I hope you know how much I love you.

Lukas, thank you for believing in me and helping this book come to life. God placed us together at a unique time and for a unique season. I couldn't be more excited for the adventures ahead.

Dad, thank you for reminding me that I'm so much more than what meets the eye. Thank you for teaching me about life—true life—and how not to be afraid. You paved the way for me in ways you couldn't even imagine. I am forever grateful.

To my beautiful wife, Ngozi, thank you for pushing me, both literally and figurately, to write and finish this book. Only you know about the long nights, early mornings, and major sacrifices made to bring this book to life. Thank you for your consistent prayer for this book, our marriage, and our children. I would not be where I am without you.

Max, thanks for always believing in me. You're the

Man. Caleb, thank you for allowing me to be your dad. Your hugs . . . your hugs have literally changed my whole outlook on life. Your kindness is unspeakable. I pray that you would continue to be a friend to all, a friend this world needs. Sophia, before you were even born, I was madly in love with you. From the time I looked at the ultrasound and saw we were having a girl you had my heart. You opened up a part of my heart that I didn't know existed. Your joy, your personality, your kisses . . . those timely kisses. You have no idea how much they mean to me.

Kelechi Victor, you came at a critical time in our lives. A time when we had to make a choice. We chose to thank God. We chose victory. We chose you.

Jenn, thank you for being there for me during some of the toughest times in my life. I can't wait to meet Joy. I'm so happy she's here! Eric, Akiem, Nick, Danny, and Trey, all of you helped me get through. I am forever grateful.

To the Nelson Books team—Ed, Sujin, Webster, Kevin, Rachel, Shea, and so many more—thank you all for believing in this book. For believing in me. Thank you for the long hours, the heavy edits, and the excellent marketing and selling of this book. I'm glad to be a part of the team!

Alex, thank you for taking my phone call. That day was one of the highlights of my life. You believed in me, and you believed in this book. I love you.

To all my coaches, teammates, managers, staff, and anyone I've come in contact with on a football field or in a locker room, thank you. Thank you for teaching me, for guiding me, and for being patient with me. Thanks for the memories. Steve Ryan! You're the Man. Thank you for being with me through this process. For being a friend. Same goes for you, Boom. You're a stud. George, it's hard to put into words what our relationship means to me. I'm so glad to call you my friend. E, you're an amazing human being. Words can't describe how much you have changed and shaped my life. I will continue to follow your lead. I love you, bro.

Mom, thank you for your everlasting kindness. You are my hero. Chichi, thank you for loving me and guiding me. You're a real one. Steph, thank you for *always* having my back. Know that I have yours. To Emeka and the rest of my extended family, your unwavering support has blown me away. I'm glad to call you my brothers and sisters.

Finally, thank you God for gifting me with your Son and your Spirit. You paid the ultimate sacrifice so that I could know you. I cannot wait to get to know you even better. Thank you.

# NOTES

1. When I came across this quote, it was attributed to Nelson Mandela's 1994 inaugural speech as the newly elected president of South Africa. Later I learned that, although often attributed to Nelson Mandela, this quote is from Marianne Williamson, *A Return to Love: Reflections on the Principles of a Course in Miracles* (New York: HarperCollins, 1992), 190–91. See "'Deepest Fear' Quote Not Mr. Mandela's," Nelson Mandela Foundation, November 9, 2017, https://www.nelsonmandela.org/news/entry/deepest-fear-quote-not-mr-mandelas/.
2. Steve Wyche, "Colin Kaepernick Explains Why He Sat During National Anthem," NFL.com, August 27, 2016, http://www.nfl.com/news/story/0ap3000000691077/article/colin-kaepernick-explains-why-he-sat-during-national-anthem.
3. Bryan Armen Graham, "Donald Trump Blasts NFL Anthem Protesters: 'Get That Son of a Bitch Off the Field,'" *Guardian*, September 23, 2017, https://www.theguardian.com/sport/2017/sep/22/donald-trump-nfl-national-anthem-protests.
4. From a conversation I had with Burl Cain the first time I visited the Louisiana State Penitentiary in March 2016. See

also "Dignity and the Moral Rehabilitation of Prisoners,"
Prison Fellowship, https://www.prisonfellowship.org/2014
/09/dignity-and-the-moral-rehabitation-of-prisoners/.

# ABOUT THE AUTHOR

Sam Acho is an author, a public speaker, a humanitarian, and a committed Christian. He is also currently a linebacker in the NFL.

He played college football at the University of Texas at Austin, where he received the William V. Campbell Trophy for being college football's top scholar-athlete. He won the NCAA Top VIII Award that recognizes the top eight student-athletes in all of sports. And he was named the 2010 Big 12 Sportsperson of the Year. In 2011, Sam was drafted by the Arizona Cardinals and played four seasons as a linebacker with the team. He then signed with the Chicago Bears for the 2015–2016 season and played four years there. He spent the 2019 season with the Tampa Bay Buccaneers.

In 2016 and 2017, Sam was the Bears' nominee for the Walter Payton NFL Man of the Year Award, the league's only award that recognizes both civic and professional contributions. He served on the leadership committee for both the Cardinals and the Bears. He is also the vice president of the NFL Players Association, an organization in which he has served since his second year in the NFL.

Having grown up in Dallas with parents who emphasized scholastic achievement, Sam was named by Sporting News as one of the twenty smartest athletes in all of sports. He received his MBA in 2015 at the Thunderbird School of Global Management, the #1 ranked international MBA program in the world.

Every year he joins his family on medical mission trips to Nigeria. He recently helped build a hospital there through Living Hope Christian Ministries, where he serves as vice president.

Sam is the founder and president of Athletes for Justice, an organization that works to unite professional athletes and everyday athletes to fight injustices around the world. He has been featured in Super Bowl commercials highlighting his social justice efforts in the city of Chicago.

Sam has spent time with such organizations as the International Justice Mission, the American Diabetes Association, and the Clinton Global Initiative. He has lobbied Congress to change laws regarding justice-related issues, both inside and outside the United States. He hosts *The Home Team* podcast and is a frequent guest on ESPN.

As a public speaker, he enjoys opportunities to encourage and inspire others to fulfill their calling by following Christ and serving others. He speaks at churches, concerts, colleges, and companies all around the world, spreading his message of hope in Christ.